Susan Bennett Fisher

Body of 9

Practices for Presence

Body-based Insight for Living a Life of Purpose

Susan Bennett Fisher

Body of 9

Practices for Presence

Body-based Insight for Living a Life of Purpose

All rights reserved. Copyright © 2021 Susan Bennett Fisher.

No part of this book may be reproduced or transmitted in any form or by any means whatsoever, including graphic, electronic, or mechanical, including photocopying, recording, taping, or by any information storage or retrieval system, without permission from the publisher.

Illustrations by Branson Faustini

Second edition: 2021

Originally Titled "9 Energies – Practices for Presence"

Printed in the United States of America

ISBN-13 978-0-9906035-6-6

Kindle Version: ISBN-13 978-0-9906035-7-3

Dedication: To all of you upon whose wisdom the foundation of this work is built – everyone we have identified, our students, advisors, teachers, our family and our friends. Without the contribution of all of you, we would not have been able to distill this wisdom. We are excited to continue this journey with you.

This book is a second edition, an updated version of our first book *9 Energies – Practices For Presence.* The original book is no longer in print.

CONTENTS:

What This Journey Holds for You 1

Section 1: Context – The Nine Natural Numbers

    Introduction to the Body of 9 5
    Chapter 1. Natural Number 1 14
    Chapter 2. Natural Number 2 18
    Chapter 3. Natural Number 3 22
    Chapter 4. Natural Number 4 26
    Chapter 5. Natural Number 5 30
    Chapter 6. Natural Number 6 34
    Chapter 7. Natural Number 7 38
    Chapter 8. Natural Number 8 42
    Chapter 9. Natural Number 9 46

Section 2: Practices for Presence and Creation

    Overview of Practices 51

  PART 1: Practices for Presence
    Chapter 10. Awaken the Observer 55
    Chapter 11. Use Curiosity to Open Awareness 68
    Chapter 12. Practice Non-Judgment 75
    Chapter 13. Hold Beliefs as Ideas and Possibilities 82

  PART 2: Practices for Creation
    Chapter 14. Clarify and State Intention 91
    Chapter 15. Practice Non-Attachment 97
    Chapter 16. Be Courageous 101
    Chapter 17. Take Wise Action 105
    Chapter 18. Choose Love 110

Conclusion 117
Glossary of Terms 119
Acknowledgements 121
About Susan Bennett Fisher 123
About Body of 9 125

What This Journey Holds for You

This book is for seekers, life-long learners, and those interested in exploring the relationship between body, mind, and spirit. There are many ways to explore how these aspects of the self relate to and work with each other, some of which—like meditation and yoga—emerged out of ancient and venerable traditions. Others rely on cutting edge science, such as the recent discovery of how our brains become healthier when we meditate regularly. What's certain, however, is that the barriers between science and spirituality, mind and body, and spirit and matter are beginning to break down.

What emerges is a more holistic way to view ourselves, one that recognizes that wisdom and knowing are not just brain or mind activities, but physical and nonphysical ones as well. Unveiled at the heart of this new understanding, which we call the Body of 9, are the nine Natural Numbers, a way to decode our own physical being that supports and contextualizes the other disciplines, philosophies, practices, models, and methods that strive to make sense out of the human experience.

Like the Enneagram or Myers Briggs Type Indicator®, Body of 9 is a system of self-discovery, but it offers something fundamentally different and actionable that virtually no other personality model provides. Body of 9 introduces the discovery that there are nine different physical presentations of the human body. We are each born with a particular region of the body that is active which shapes our perceptions, skills and gifts, we call this your Natural Number.

This book provides an overview of the nine Natural Numbers and gives you a starting place—a set of specific Practices for Presence and Creation—to help you develop your innate and natural wisdom. The information that follows will teach you how to begin to create a new context for your life experience, whether or not you know your Natural Number. Just acknowledging that the person in front of you is not operating on the same frequency, not receiving the same information, and is driven by vastly different motivations that stem from their body creates a level of appreciation, understanding, and acceptance.

If you know your Natural Number...
You will gain additional insight into your own Natural Number, and those of the other eight. You will learn to dance more easily with your own power and others'. Supported by the knowledge of your Natural Number, you will discover and develop practices designed to help you fulfill your true potential in this lifetime.

If you are as yet unaware of your Natural Number[1]...
You will gain a foundational understanding of the transformative power of the Body of 9, while being challenged in your thinking of how you see yourself and others. As you explore the Practices for Presence and Creation, you will also discover ways to awaken your deeper body wisdom in service of living a purpose-filled life.

Wherever we find ourselves on the path of transformation, knowledge of the Natural Numbers can embolden and energize our daily practice, showing us how to use our natural abilities to create fresh outcomes and open ourselves to change, growth, and transformation. It's as if they serve as a fresh wind, blowing away our old beliefs and enlivening the work of our spirits. The truth is, our bodies are equipped to perceive information, contained as energy, in the world around us. By using our innate ability to sense vibrations and interpret the information at nine different frequencies, we discover a new way to unlock the mysteries of the human experience. As Nikola Tesla said, "To find the secrets of the universe you have to think in terms of energy, frequency, and vibration."

---

[1] See the website bodyof9.com to find out where and when you can have your Natural Number Identified by a Body of 9 Practitioner.

Body of 9 is the organization that I run with my husband, Martin Fisher. Over the years, from small gatherings in our living room to hundreds-strong festivals and conferences, we've identified the Natural Number of over eight thousand people, of fifty nationalities and almost all races. This experience with people has taught us that the consistency and similarity of people who share a Natural Number is *greater* than that of people who share culture, race, or gender. At some level, we may have more in common in how we perceive the world and what we care about with a Bushman in Africa with whom we share a Natural Number than with our spouse, parent, or sibling who will have a different Natural Number. In other words, our Natural Number is a significant force in shaping our identity and perceptions.

When my youngest daughter was asked why she lost interest in science, she answered, "Everything that we know and believe to be true, be it science, religion, philosophy, anything, is based on a set of assumptions, and when you expand those assumptions out, look at the beliefs and conjectures that underlie the obvious, you actually approach the infinite."

Ultimately, then, this book is about learning to look beyond your limiting beliefs and unexamined assumptions in order to connect to your infinite being, the part of you that is in touch with your deepest purpose. It is a journey that requires you to enter with a beginner's mind, to feel and experience with an open heart. Until you reach the end of the book, and have explored some of the Practices described along the way, it is best to suspend judgment. In the case of this work, embodied practice is truly the best test of efficacy.

One final word: please don't choose to disbelieve, at least until you have had your own experience with your Natural Number. You may find, as I did, that it rocks your world, helping you to unlock the key to your joy, power, and purpose.

SECTION 1:
Context — The Body of 9

Introduction to the Body of 9

You are hopefully familiar with some of your physical senses: sight, hearing, taste, smell, and touch. You also may be aware of balance, pressure, temperature, and pain. But very few among us know that there are nine additional senses that provide us information in the physical realm.

Unlike our physical senses, however, only one natural sense is active in our bodies from birth. We refer to this as the Natural Number. We call the particular region of the body that is active in us from birth the Natural Number Region. Each of us has a Natural Number that we liken to a Superpower – it is so strong that it flavors all of our life experiences, and even influences how our body develops. It is the primary lens we use to perceive and experience everything and everyone else.

Without developing our conscious connection and awareness of how to work with our Natural Number, our true potential is rarely easily accessible. The existence of our Natural Number is not widely known or recognized; it is overlooked, and not supported in us from birth. Over time, we lose touch with the innate power that is born into us. We cannot access it consciously unless we actually know it exists.

Most people have had some experience of stumbling into the activation of their own Natural Number. When we are "in the zone," experiencing times of creativity, heightened performance, or deep intimacy that mark the magical moments of our lives, our Natural Number has kicked into action and opened a space for our being to lead. These experiences are usually quite profound, even overwhelming, and yet most people have no way of consciously recreating them, unless they know how to tap into their Natural Number.

Knowing your Natural Number and actively practicing its activation gives you a way to access your strength and power at will. Our Natural Number affects how we interact with other people, how we experience both our physical and spiritual nature, and even how we move; that's why it is sometimes referred to as your Superpower. Finding your Natural Number is like Superman donning his Superman outfit, or Dorothy in the Wizard of Oz clicking her ruby slippers together. It's magic, yet it's grounded and real, all at the same time. It transforms you into the Superhero you were meant to be.

Our Natural Number communicates to the world around us, physically and energetically. People are physically shaped by their Natural Number. This can be seen in the:

- **Natural Number Region:** Each Natural Number initiates movement from a particular region of the body, comprised of skeletal structures, muscles, and fascia related to the location of the Natural Number. It influences the style and manner in which our bodies move.

- **Facial Expression of Activation:** Each Natural Number has a distinct facial expression, which includes the way in which the eyes work and a particular quality of expression, created by the shape, muscular hold, and movement of the cheeks and mouth.[2]

- **Energy Signature of Activation:** Each Natural Number, when stimulated in the body, has a particular energetic impact or signature that other people can feel.

- **Activation Posture:** Each of the Natural Numbers has a primary physical posture which assists with the activation

---

[2] The Facial Expressions of Activation, naturally occurring phenomena in the human body, were first noticed by New Equations®.

of the Natural Number Region. These postures can be used to identify which Region is most active in a person.[3]

- **Physiological Body Structure:** The senses, eyes, and musculature of our faces, heads, chests, and lower bodies develop differently depending on which Natural Number is most active.

Your Natural Number is the Most Influential Force in Shaping how your Body Develops and who you Become

Your Natural Number determines how you move. We all initiate our movement from our Activation Region. When people move in harmony with their nature, it feels highly supportive of the body and it can be very beautiful to witness.

Your Natural Number impacts how you interact with other people. For example, those with Natural Numbers 1, 2, 3, and 4 use their eyes as part of the relationship-connection creation process, to actively build a specific type of relationship related to their Natural Number. Those with Natural Numbers 5 through 9, conversely, do not use direct eye contact as part of the activation of their Natural Number, they use them to observe.

Your Natural Number impacts how you interact with Source or Spirit, or whatever you call that energy that surrounds us and is greater than us. Each Natural Number connects and interacts with a different aspect of Source energy in a completely different way. For example, Natural Number 7 connects to infinite wisdom. Natural Number 6 feels the Source energy present in everything that exists.

---

[3] Some Activation Postures were originally identified by New Equations but have evolved due to Body of 9 research and development.

How each Natural Number experiences the world is explained more in depth in the following Natural Number specific chapters.

Your Natural Number is reflected in your face and body. Each of the Natural Numbers has a particular expression that shows when active. The quality in the eyes and the facial muscular hold is impacted by the active Region, and indicates which Natural Number is present. Body structure also varies depending on your Natural Number. For example, people of Natural Number 6 have expanded and lifted rib cages, and a relatively flat and firm sternum. People of Natural Number 9 have a wider and more open upper chest area, and more developed musculature along the spine, most visible when the arms are set back in the Natural Number 9 Posture of Activation. These distinct physiological differences are part of what we use to discern a person's Natural Number.

Your Natural Number also affects how you take in and process information. If you are exploring the activation the other energies, your senses function according to which Region is active. For example, the eyes of someone with Natural Number 3 have a much greater ability to focus and narrow in, so that they view their surroundings in a much more concentrated way. Those with Natural Number 5 have a 360-degree awareness, which allows them to hear and follow what is going on all around them. What we perceive in our environment is shaped by the region or Natural Number that is activated.

And here is the paradox: each person brings their unique wisdom into the world, and it is both focused on and sourced from the activation of their Natural Number in the body. This wisdom best achieves its universal relevance when understood in the context of all nine Natural Numbers.

You can learn how to activate the other eight Natural Numbers, first by teaching your body the muscular and skeletal position associated with each Natural Number; next, it requires letting go of your own Natural Number and surrendering to an unfamiliar yet equally powerful part of your body. Simultaneously move your body and apply a conscious intention to activate that Natural Number region. This can be an uncomfortable, eye-opening.

Having this experience is an immensely powerful indication of the differences between us. With the activation of the other eight Natural Numbers within your body awareness, activation and control of your Natural Number becomes easier and better understood as well. When one can activate all nine Natural Numbers consciously at will, the synergy and wisdom of the Body of 9 becomes available.

Gifts and Wisdom of the Natural Numbers

When we understand the world's wisdom in the context of nine Natural Numbers, we are more discerning about the source of the information and can more easily decide if we want to integrate that wisdom into our current growth cycle. For example, if a particular teacher of meditation has Natural Number 5, their impact will be very different than that of a meditation taught by someone with Natural Number 7, or any of the other Natural Numbers. It may or may not resonate with you in this moment or the next.

Learning about the nine Natural Numbers, whether you know your Natural Number or not, helps you to understand the nine, different, embodied ways in which people show up and experience the world. How you perceive the wisdom of others and how you share your innate wisdom is deeply connected to the nine Natural Numbers.

Each **Natural Number** offers a particular gift in community. **Your** presence alone brings the impact and benefit of **your** Natural Number to each person in the community. The nine together—when consciously contributed—are designed to function as a working whole:

- **Natural Number 1** connects to energy from the Source of creation, aligning all present to their Source-level selves.

- **Natural Number 2** creates the connection needed for each of us to hear, receive, and respond to one another.

- **Natural Number 3** activates our soul, enabling us to give our gift from our highest purpose.

- **Natural Number 4** connects us into the place where we are all connected, the Source of life, so we remember that when we create, it must be done in alignment with who we are as a collective and as individuals.

- **Natural Number 5** helps us know what is known and what we need to find out; to know where we are and what is possible from what we already know.

- **Natural Number 6** energizes the transformation process and moves the community forward in the most alive direction.

- **Natural Number 7** ensures that we let go of what is not of service and remain open to new possibilities. They hold the larger vision for the community.

- **Natural Number 8** enables us to use the power of our bodies and the earth to protect, nurture, and support the growth needed to bring the transformation to fruition.

- **Natural Number 9** helps to bring the human process to conclusion, metabolize the experience, and free the energy of the transformation process to begin again in a way that includes everything.

The presence of all nine Natural Numbers is required to enable the transformation process to function optimally. If any Natural Number is missing, their function cannot be executed by any person with a different Natural Number. In the world today, it is very rare that all nine Natural Numbers are included in a community. Even in situations where all nine are present, we are so focused on our individuality that we are not optimally able to hear and include the wisdom of the other eight Natural Numbers.

Our Natural Number dramatically impacts every aspect of our experience. When someone says, "I know how you feel," in an attempt to show empathy or find common ground, eight out of nine times they really don't have any idea what a person is experiencing.

Every aspect of existence is influenced by how our body takes in information. We receive information, and then translate, decode, and make sense of it according to our Natural Number's Activation Region. Then we transmit back our new understanding from the experience—our inherent wisdom—to others, again through our body's Activation Region. Most of the time, we are not aware that we are doing this, and others are not consciously aware of the wisdom and gifts they are receiving.

The Activation Posture

Without conscious experience of how to activate one's Natural Number by knowing where it is centered in the body, what posture activates it, and what it feels like, it is challenging to recreate that feeling of "rightness" that is possible when we're in the flow of our Natural Number.

Like many, you have probably experienced this for yourself, wondering why something felt so amazingly right on one occasion, and then fell flat on another. And while there are many spiritual and personal growth practices designed to help us back into that flow, they are missing the physical context of the nine Natural Numbers—the nine different presentations of the human body. Therefore, those practices are only effective if they serendipitously happen to support your particular Natural Number. For example, a certain yoga or meditation position might offer the perfect physical gesture to activate your Natural Number. It wasn't the intention of the pose, but the benefit is real nonetheless.

When we activate our own Natural Number through postural adjustment and attention, we consciously heighten our own super-powered "sixth sense" experience of the world. Effectively, it allows us to switch on our Observer at will, and begin the transformational process. As we observe our own behavior from our new viewpoint, we find our behavior changing. These changes shift the course of our lives and assist us in creating a new reality.

Holding the body in a physical posture that supports the flow of spiritual energy is critical to developing awareness of—and ability to use—one's own Natural Number and the other eight. By consciously creating new habits for how to hold our bodies, we begin to access hidden information. Our bodies are designed to tap into the field of spiritual energy that contains everything that is known and everything that is unknowable. Our realities are formed from a combination of knowledge, experience, and Source energy that is perceivable only when our Natural Number is active.

When we learn to shift our posture to experience all nine Natural Numbers, we begin to feel the flow of the spiritual energy through the body. This provides new information that helps us to align with our greater purpose, create deep and sustaining relationships, calm the mind, metabolize emotions, and move forward in ways that benefit all.

If you have ever watched a truly stunning performance, the performer most certainly tapped into their Natural Number, whether they were aware of it or not. In turn, we are attracted to the beauty of a person whose Natural Number is flowing out into the world. When a person is performing at a high level, we see evidence of their Natural Number's magic through their posture of activation, which includes the Facial Expression of Activation as well as movements that stem from their Activation Region.

If you know your Natural Number, you learned about the physical position in which your body is strongest. People tend to put the region associated with their Natural Number in advance of other parts of the body. Thus, someone with Natural Number 4 might walk around with the pelvis slightly tilted forward, while someone of Natural Number 5 might walk with the head down, pointing the top of the head forward.

The activated region of our Natural Number leads our movement. Over time, we develop unconscious body habits to either project or protect our Natural Number. This means there is either a collapse around the Natural Number region, or it is projected outward. Both tendencies, when not understood in the context of the Natural Number, lead to shifts and changes in our posture that may block or change the flow of energy in the body.

We have all been told to sit up straight, and many of us bemoan our poor posture. Everywhere you turn, there are resources for properly aligning your body. It turns out that proper alignment of the body helps the health of the physical body, the flow of spiritual energy, and the vibrancy of the Natural Numbers in your body.

The following chapters on each Natural Number offer a brief but focused overview and a description of how to activate the body. Each chapter uses the language we have been offered by people of that Natural Number to describe their experience of reality. The description of the other Natural Numbers may not make sense to you, but the one of your Natural Number should be clear and comprehensible.

Chapter 1.
Natural Number 1

Natural Number 1 (NN1)

Natural Number 1 (NN1) is about experiencing the Source[4] and **value** in others, as well as using Source in relationships to feel, see, and share the awe, beauty and majesty of the world and the people within it. Deeply honoring and respecting others derives from this experience of Source.

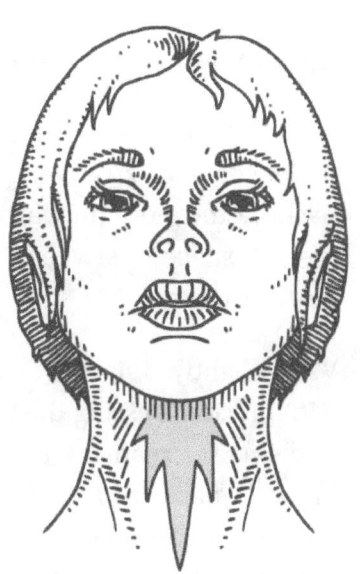

Natural Number 1's activated region is at the top of the neck **under the chin**, in the Hyoglossus, and the other muscles under the chin.

People with NN1 describe being directly connected to Source or Spirit. Encountering something awe-inspiring in nature, like a magnificent sunrise or sunset, triggers a remembering of that connection to Source in each of us, and is experienced as awe. People of NN1 connect at will with that sense of beauty, wonder, and majesty in anything, and they are most energized and fulfilled when in that space of appreciation and awe.

As Source enters their being, activating their Nature, they are able to share the beauty and perfection of existence with us through gentle, honoring, eye-to-eye contact.

In this honoring connection, people of Natural Number 1 enable you to know that you are made from and connected to Source, and through this you can know the beauty and perfection of each other.

---

[4] Source is used in this book to refer to the power of creation, the Cosmic Energy that creates life. This can mean different things to different people. Please feel free to use whatever word or concept you would like to substitute that is in alignment with your beliefs. See the Glossary of Terms to better understand the intent of the word Source with respect to the definition.

Knowing this infinite connection to Source, we can all experience the majesty of creation in the moment, in whatever is before us.

Natural Number 1 Activation Posture:

Focus on the top of the neck, under the chin, stretching the back of the neck upward to create space between the neck vertebrae.

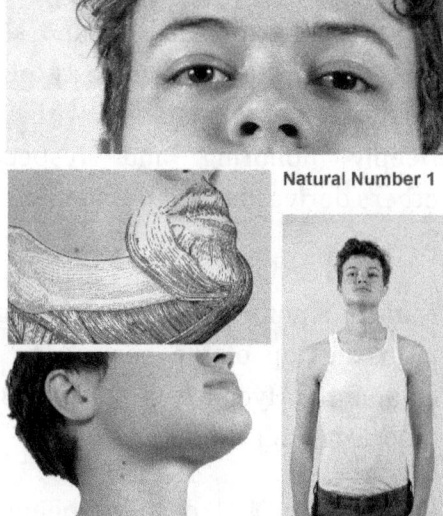

Natural Number 1

Very slightly raise the chin without compressing the back of the neck, creating a tension in the Hyoglossus muscle, the muscle at the base of the tongue, and the other muscles under the chin.

Continue to bring your attention to the area under the chin; the muscles there will tighten and the chin will move very slightly forward as Natural Number 1 activates. Allow the eyes to soften. If you are making eye contact with someone, do your best to blink as little as possible, allow yourself to give over to the connection as you receive and send Source energy from the underside of the chin.

Core Values for Natural Number 1s:

Appreciation: NN1s intrinsically know the value of beauty, people, life, and circumstances. They recognize the changing nature of creation and appreciate its harmony and balance.

Acceptance: NN1s love people as they are, where they are, and who they are. They know that people are doing the best they can with where they are right now. They know deep in their being that all people are equal and should be honored.

Connection: NN1s value deep sustained connection at the level of the essence of life. They recognize and connect with the essence of our being, inviting and enabling us to understand our existence. They value being fully present to the connection with you in this infinite moment.

Creativity: NN1s are driven to express their understanding of Source, beauty, and value through their creative powers. This can be in any medium or talent they choose.

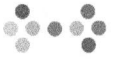

Chapter 2.
Natural Number 2

Natural Number 2 (NN2)

Natural Number 2 (NN2) is about connection through relationships to the magic in others. It is a merging with others, attuning with our whole being to the body of another person for the sake of connection alone. Natural Number 2 teaches us that we must start everything with connection through active engagement.

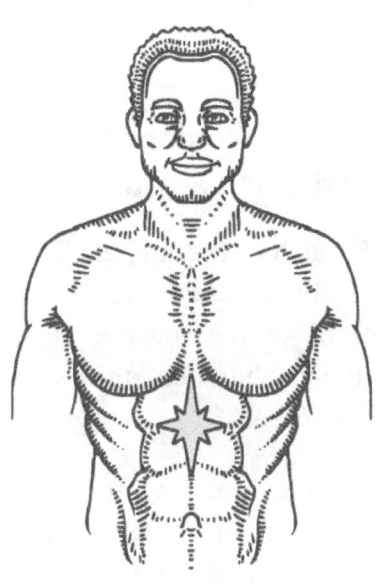

Natural Number 2's Activation Region is at the Upper Rectus Abdominus, also known as the top third of the abs or "six-pack."

People with this Natural Number connect to others so powerfully that they liken it to an energetic entanglement. Meeting another person, we often experience an exchange when our energetic signatures interact with each other. For many, this initial interaction can be uncomfortable. Those with Natural Number 2, however, experience no energetic conflict or need for negotiation; they simply shift their energetic signature to synchronize and resonate with another.

In this engagement, people with **Natural Number** 2 experience the world through your reality, allowing them to know how to support you and be with you. They only want you to be yourself, in the moment, and to stay engaged with them. Experiencing connection with people of **Natural Number** 2 helps us know that being in connection with others is good and right.

Through connection, they sense what others need, and provide it in whatever way is most appropriate. They experience the importance of creating and holding connection with others, almost as a physical pressure.

Natural Number 2 Activation Posture:

Focus on the Upper Rectus Abdominus muscles, the top third of the muscles in the upper abdomen, the top of the "6-pack".

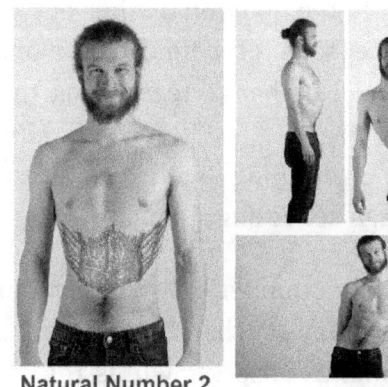

Expand and tighten these muscles. The lower abdomen comes in to support the lift and expansion of the upper muscle. Eye contact can be included; it begins in a neutral place, and as the connection **happens** the eyes

Natural Number 2

will naturally begin to brighten in engagement. Keep attention on the Upper Abs as the connection grows. Allow yourself to feel and respond using this part of the body.

Movement is part of Natural Number 2 as well. When activating your NN2 in engagement with another person, you may want to include movement and allow your body to respond to the person in front of you.

Core Values for Natural Number 2s:

Engagement: They offer an invitation to be fully present in the connection; nothing else matters in that moment. They are looking for meaningful engagement.

Dynamic Harmony: It is important to people with **Natural Number 2** to create dynamic harmony through the connection. They are able to adjust to and enliven the connection with another person, as the person changes dynamically through the interaction.

Movement: Through movement, both at the cellular and muscular level, they understand what a person needs, how to be with them, and how to engage in the relationship. They have a personal need to be moving, which creates a sense of being alive. Movement in dynamic harmony with the world is a **Natural Number** 2's way of interacting.

Chapter 3.
Natural Number 3

Natural Number 3 (NN3)

Natural Number 3 (NN3) is about a focused connection to others that ignores the persona and goes straight to our being, our greater purpose, and using the joy of connection from that relationship to inspire others into action toward that purpose.

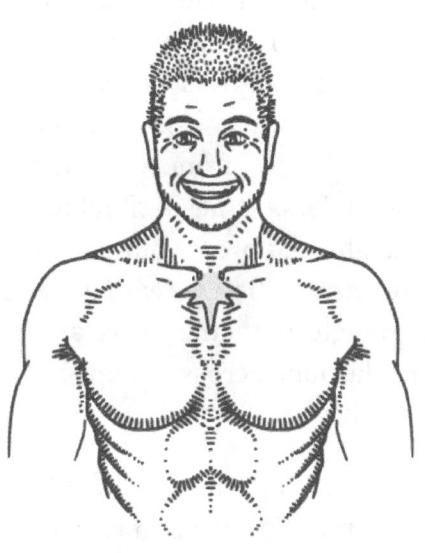

Natural Number 3's Activation Region is at the top of the sternum—at the Sternal Notch on the Manubrium—supported by the top rib that connects to T1 on the spine **and stretches across the clavicle.** The activation also includes a full smile that goes all the way into the eyes and emanates from deep inside, where the joy of the soul resides.

This activation enables people of NN3 to inspire us to take action from the innately guided part of ourselves. When someone with NN3 activates, their soul fills with joy, energizing them, lighting up their eyes and their smile; in turn, they share this joy with you enlivening and energizing you toward the vision they see for you.

When they look into your eyes, they see through your ego-masks, connecting instead to your deepest self. They energize you by shining joy and light into your being. This connection empowers your being to speak out and creates a profound sense of inner delight, inspiring you to move forward from your best intentions and highest purpose.

Natural Number 3
Activation Posture

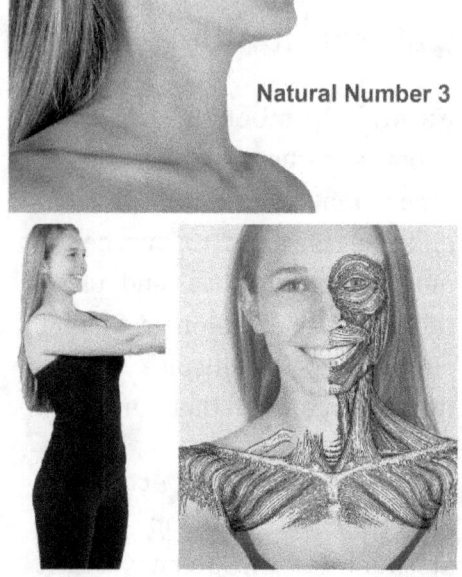

Natural Number 3

Focus on using the upper Trapezius muscles to lift the upper sternum. One of the ways to do this is to put your arms locked-out straight from your shoulders, at shoulder height, and press your palms together flat creating a triangle with the arms and collarbone across the upper-chest.

As you press your hands together this makes it easier to **lift** up across the collarbone. The lift comes from the Manubrium at the top of the sternum, below the clavicle.

Choose something on which to focus, preferably another person. As you make eye contact, keep the lift high and your focus sharp. Feel into yourself, allowing your inside joy to bubble up and shine through your eyes, and smile.

When those with **Natural Number** 3 lift the Manubrium using the upper Trapezius muscles at the shoulders, it lifts the collarbone, making it higher and more pronounced. Most NN3s have collarbones that protrude on either side of the manubrium.

Core Values for Natural Number 3:

Generosity: NN3s use the energy of generosity to power the connection with others. By generously giving from the deepest part of themselves, they are able to activate us without agenda.

Drive: NN3s have an internal compulsion to share the energy of essence and creation with others. This creates a driving excitement, magic, and intensity that moves everything forward.

Connection through Focus: Using focus to create the big picture from small details is a great strength of NN3s. They are able to gather the deeper meaning in the energy of the tiniest particulars, and build a more inspiring, understanding vision for what is possible. They can then direct that energy toward the possibility that they see for others.

Chapter 4.
Natural Number 4

Natural Number 4 (NN4)

Natural Number 4 (NN4) is about our relationship to our infinite self, to our life-force within our being. Through knowing and accepting our timeless selves, we are ready to transform using our connection to our deepest life force energy.

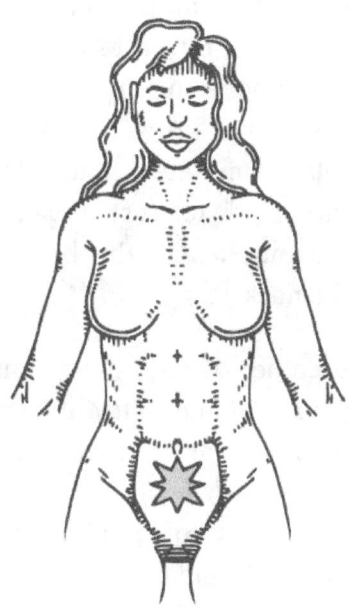

Natural Number 4's Activation Region uses the muscles of the lower abdomen. People of NN4 use audible breath—both in and out—to descend into their internal selves, the place where there is but one infinite Life Force.

Once they reach that warm, safe, and comfortable space, they can include us, making us feel like we are in a protective bubble. They fill the bubble with a warm, rich feeling, almost as if a secret love potion were seeping into your being. This experience provides a deep sense of intimacy, and helps us know that we not alone.

Inside this bubble you are also connected to your inner self. Since our inner selves are infinite and timeless, we remember that we are sacred beings. We accept that who and where we are now is how and where we are meant to be in this moment. We remember our past is the gift we have been given to allow us to move forward, without carrying our past as baggage. Instead, our past becomes a foundation for the person we are growing into and becoming.

When we feel our infinite self, we know that we live a paradox of being a part of the whole while manifested here in life as separate individuals.

Natural Number 4 Activation Posture

Bring attention to the lower abdominal muscles, making them taut and pushing them outward by rotating the pubic bone forward and up. Allow the upper body to relax completely, and allow the head to rest, relaxing the muscles in the back of the neck.

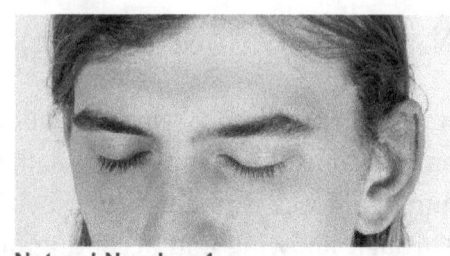
Natural Number 4

Breathe deeply down into your abdomen, allowing your breath to grow audible and the muscles of the lower abdomen to guide your breath, in and out.

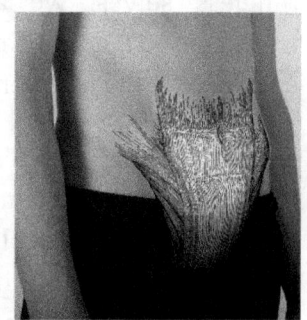

As you breathe in, allow your attention to drop more deeply inside, expanding the lower abdomen to accommodate the breath rather than expanding the chest. As you breathe out, feel your lower abdomen push outward, drawing your attention ever deeper inside.

This can be done when you are alone, or when you are with another person. It can be done with your eyes shut or open. It is most effective, however, to do this alone when first practicing, perhaps lying down or sitting, with the eyes closed.

If you are doing this with another person, feel your abdomen expand out to include them in your bubble; allow the warm, rich feeling inside you to envelope the other person.

Core Values for NN4s

Alignment and Authenticity: NN4s value, generate, and use alignment to create authenticity. By settling into the lower abdomen, they drop into the deep and intimate space of self, which creates a sense of alignment and thereby safety.

They share that experience of alignment and acceptance through connection with others. This creates space for others to show up authentically in the moment.

The Process: NN4s understand how our pace is part of our wisdom. They move at the speed of emotional knowing. They understand that achieving deep alignment with self takes a process at a meandering pace. As water flows with gravity, so does our awareness of self, always – in the end – finding the deepest place within the body.

Connection: NN4s connect deeply through their lower abdomen to themselves, and then out to the people around them. This creates a sense of deep intimacy, a knowing of others, and an understanding of the emotional content and wisdom contained in the connection.

Chapter 5.
Natural Number 5

Natural Number 5 (NN5)

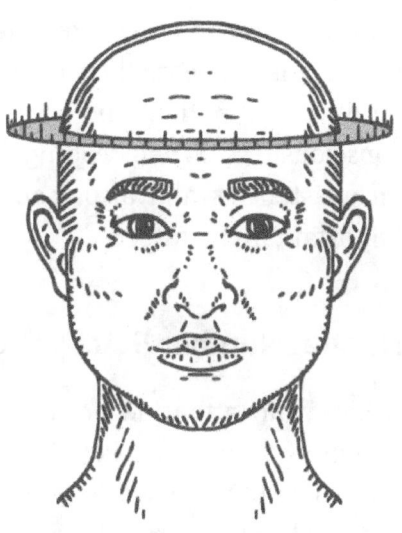

Natural Number 5 (NN5) sets and holds the context for transformation—what do we know, what do we need to find out, how is what we know related to everything else and what are the relationships that need to be taken into account?

NN5s evaluate what they learn in the context of what they know. This enables them to find inconsistencies and evaluate information to determine accuracy and importance. They help others to understand what is happening and what it means, **they know** how everything is interconnected.

Natural Number 5's Activation Region is the back and top of the head, essentially encompassing the Parietal bone of the skull, or the crown of the head. By elevating the Superior Temporal Line, thereby creating the sensation of an opening in the crown of the head, the entire skull expands.

People of NN5 have a 360-degree awareness of the world around them. They can perceive over a wide range and space. They build a visual map of their surroundings and know what is located where. They help others know where they are orienting in time and space.

Using intuition, their ability to read other's body, and their experiences, NN5s make sense of what is new in the context of what is known to help us understand where we stand and what to pay attention to as we move forward to choose the best outcome for all concerned.

People with NN5 hold virtual models of reality in their consciousness; the model shows what they know and what is missing or needs exploration. Given a vision or goal, sparked by input, Natural Number 5 helps us navigate to our destination. Natural Number 5 removes the fog of uncertainty. When the way forward is unclear, they chart possible options and paths using intuition, empathy, and by connecting to humanity's flow of consciousness. When reading or listening, people with NN5 detect inconsistencies and also mentally "flag" information that will be important in the future.

Natural Number 5 Activation Posture

Bring your attention to the crown of your head. Position the crown of the head directly over the shoulders. Extend upward, leading with the crown, allowing space to be created between the cervical vertebrae. Relax the whole body as if suspended from your crown. Feel the Temporalis muscles on the side of the head lift upward.

Close your eyes if your environment is causing a distraction, or keep them open with relaxed, open focus. Notice your hearing expand to 360-degree awareness.

The sensation is that of holding your head in space, creating a connection to the spiritual world from your head and the physical world with your body.

Imagine an infinite lake of power above your head and pull that power down into your spine.

Core Values for Natural Number 5s

Interconnectedness: NN5s know that all knowledge and experience is interconnected, and can be held in the context of everything that is both known and, as yet, unknown.

Congruence: NN5s look for congruence in what they know and learn. When they receive information that is not congruent, this sets off alarm bells, and the information cannot be added to their map of understanding until – and if – it becomes congruent.

Understanding: NN5s believe that, ultimately, anything can be known, given time and access. This creates a great patience, coupled with a deep curiosity and thirst for knowledge. They are driven to understand both the physical and the nonphysical aspects of our human experience.

Curiosity: NN5s are naturally curious; they are constantly following the breadcrumbs to find the most interesting and relevant information to create new interconnections and leaps of understanding.

Chapter 6.
Natural Number 6

Natural Number 6 (NN6)

Natural Number 6 (NN6) points us in the most alive direction, providing the energy necessary for movement to overcome any inherent inertia.

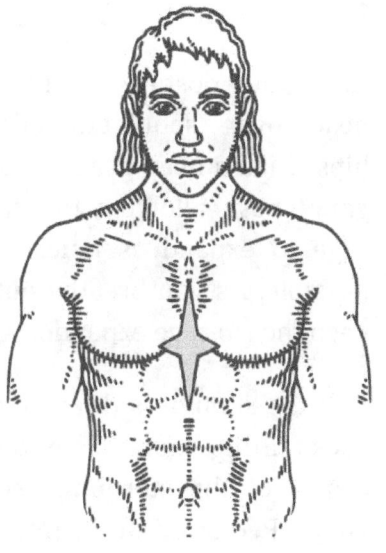

People with this Natural Number experience the spiritual energy present in a community, then decode and magnify it back, so everyone can tap into the infinite energy of creation.

Natural Number 6's Activation Region is the ribcage and chest. They expand the Inter-Costal muscles between the ribs of the chest and raise the Sternum, creating a tension that allows their chest to feel **like a drum with which they** read the vibration of the spiritual energy in the world around them.

Our combined intentions, experiences, wishes, and desires create a Universal Field of energy. People with NN6 are able to read the energy of the Universal Field[5] and move a community or person in the direction indicated by the Universal Will. By taking in the energy of each person and the environment, they are able to know what the community needs and wants to happen. From this powerful foundation, they move us to action, taking what is static and turning it dynamic.

Those with NN6 experience the incredible magic of being alive; they are able to tap the vibrancy of the energy contained in

---

[5] Universal Field is defined in the Glossary of Terms.

everything around them and magnify this energy out to others in any community in which they are participating, so that others can feel it too.

Natural Number 6 Activation Posture

Align your posture naturally, head over shoulders over hips. Take a deep breath into your chest, allowing the rib cage to expand as much as possible. As you breathe out, keep the rib cage expanded.

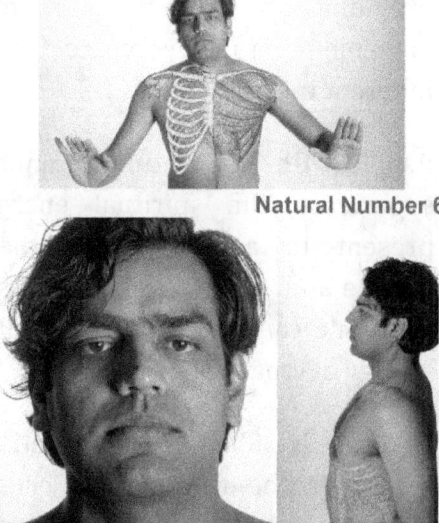

Natural Number 6

Roll the shoulders down and back, lifting more from the center of the sternum. Feel your Pectoral and Intercostal muscles—the muscles in between the ribs—engage and expand to support the lift in your chest, further stretching it into a drum like state. Expand more with each breath; hold the expansion as you continue to breathe.

Notice your awareness expand as a sense of energetic acuity raises your awareness to the nature of the world around you. It can feel **both** peaceful and incredibly alive.

This creates a waiting place where you receive the information from the Universal Field, the community, or the person in front of you. When moved to speak or act, do so in alignment with the energy you are receiving.

Core Values for Natural Number 6:

Significance: NN6s can feel what is true and present in the energy of the moment; this creates a sense of significance, a knowing of what is important and alive. They care deeply about expressing the current moment's wisdom when it is of value to the person or community present.

Aliveness: NN6s feel what is most "alive" in the current energetic space, and will focus on moving it into action. If something is not alive, it is not as interesting to a person of NN6, and often they do not know where to go with it. Aliveness can be a fleeting thing; NN6s are always responding to the **continual** changes in energy around them.

Action: NN6s thrive on action. They truly love to do things, and get things done. The sense of accomplishment is very rewarding to people of NN6. When truth and aliveness come together to become significant, NN6s are compelled into action.

What is Next: NN6s are always looking for what is next, and wait in the present moment until they make sense of the energetic answer. This is not about planning for the future; it is about the next response in the next moment, driven by what is currently happening.

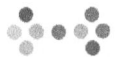

Chapter 7.
Natural Number 7

Natural Number 7 (NN7)

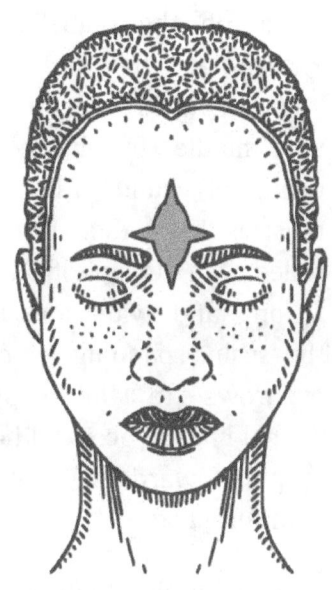

Natural Number 7 (NN7) is about purpose and possibility. People of this Natural Number see the unique purpose of a person, group, or community, and they can present possibilities that have not yet been envisioned that will move those involved toward their greatest purpose.

They also enable us to leave behind that which no longer serves us to ensure that we can move forward toward our great vision and stay open to what we do not yet know. Change is inherent in transformation; NN7 helps us let go of what no longer serves, thereby creating space to open to new possibility.

Natural Number 7's Activation Region is the Glabella, the flattened triangular elevation of the frontal bone located at the center of the forehead just above the brow line, often referred to as the third eye; this Region also involves the Frontalis muscles on the side of the forehead, which pull the scalp back.

People of NN7 have access to infinite possibilities. This can be in the form of ideas, options, and visions. They care deeply about people achieving the potential they see in them. They might even risk their relationship with you to make sure you understand what you are capable of, and how you can know, reach, and fulfill your greater purpose. People with NN7 also have the ability to create, lead, and inspire a community to achieve a grander vision.

Natural Number 7
Activation Posture

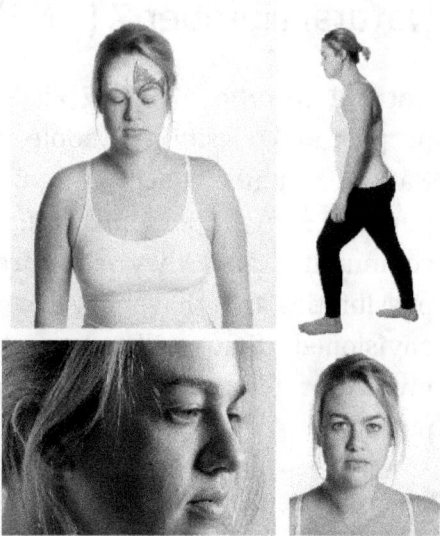

Natural Number 7

Focus on the Glabella, also known at the Third Eye; you can touch it gently with the middle finger of your dominant hand. Allow the muscles on the forehead, called the Occipitofrontalis, a long and wide muscle of the scalp, spanning from the eyebrows to the superior nuchal lines of occipital bones, to pull toward the center of your forehead.

Allow your chin to drop and tuck in toward your neck while closing your eyes; allow your eyes to rotate in to look up at the Glabella.

Keep your focus on the space just behind the Glabella, emptying your mind completely and creating stillness. Wait in the stillness until insight, new information, and new possibility presents itself. It may feel like a pressure on the Glabella.

Core Values for Natural Number 7:

Freedom: People with NN7 value freedom for themselves and others – the freedom to experience adventure, to open to where vision, curiosity, and intuition can take you into the unexplored. This may show up as a resistance to boundaries, status quo, and rules.

Fun and Adventure: Fun and adventure are staples to people with NN7. The experience of exploring their world can be highly entertaining. In that space, they can be very adaptable to the ideas and possibilities that present themselves.

Possibility: People with NN7 value staying open to possibility, exploring different directions, and seeing where curiosity leads. They help us stay receptive to possibilities that have not yet entered the realm of the known.

Truth: NN7s need to know it is safe to be honest with you, and they want you to be honest with them. They don't need or want a sugar coating of truth; they want to be able to tell you how they see things in the present moment **without fear of judgement.**

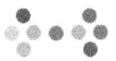

Chapter 8.
Natural Number 8

Natural Number 8 (NN8)

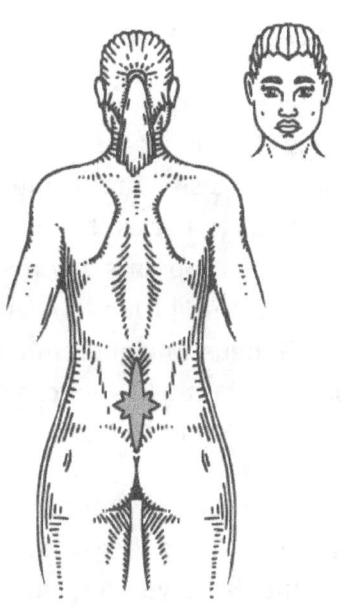

Natural Number 8 (NN8) guides us to move forward together to create with consideration and integrity for the benefit of all. Aligning the body with the physical source of creation, they draw energy from the earth. This guides them to create an atmosphere ripe for growth and change.

Natural Number 8's Activation Region is located at the base of the spine, at the sacrum, and is activated by tilting the sacrum toward the ground and clenching the Gluteus Maximus muscles downward, causing the sacrum to align to support the spine. NN8 bodies connect down into the earth and draw energy and power from the earth. Their physical self is the same as their soul-self.

They use this earth/spirit-based connection to define gentleness power and integrity. From this place of body integrity and supreme gentleness, they can heal what needs healing and manifest growth and creation. Keeping all in a place of internal, natural integrity, they have a heightened body awareness that goes down to the cellular level. Essentially, they know and teach that our spiritual nature—our soul—is contained in every cell of our body.

This level of awareness of both the power and the gentleness needed to create integrity allows them to feel what needs to be done, in what order, and by whom; they also know how to do all of this with safety, taking everyone into account with gentleness, and in a way that will endure. People with Natural Number 8 inherently know how to use the combined energy of a community to create sustainable structure.

Natural Number 8 Activation Posture

Either standing or sitting, bring your focus to the sacrum; use the Gluteous Maximus muscles to tilt the sacrum so it points downward toward the ground, keeping the Gluteus Maximus muscles of your buttocks clenched to hold you firmly in place.

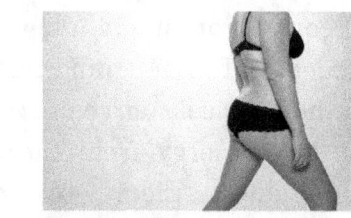

Natural NUMBER 8

Feel the energy extend down through your legs to the ground, as if you are pushing into the ground. It might feel like your feet grow roots into the earth. Allow your upper body and jaw to relax.

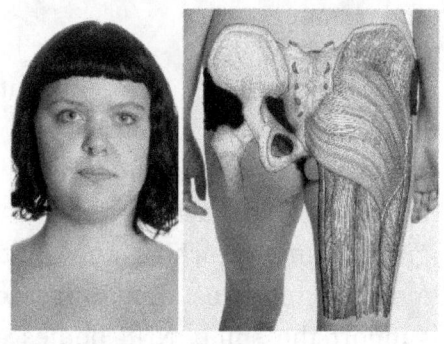

The upper body is perched and relaxed on the sacrum. This creates a deeper awareness of your body, its connection to the earth, and the flow of energy up and down.

Core Values for Natural Number 8:

Trust: NN8s value trust. There are three parts of what trust means for NN8s: 1) they need to feel trusted by others, giving them a sense of purpose and value; 2) in relationships, trust means that all people take responsibility for their part of the process, i.e. say what they will do and do what they say; and 3) there is also the component of trusting their body and listening to the wisdom it provides.

Loyalty: NN8s value loyalty in all meaningful relationships. Loyalty grows out of the relationship, as trust builds. NN8s are loyal as a part of friendship. This shows up as a strong feeling of support or allegiance for people they trust.

Integrity in the Body: For NN8s, everything goes through the body. Because of their hyper-awareness of the body, sensations and feelings inform them of what is going on, what is important and, if needed, what should be done. They know that they need to pay attention to what their body signals.

Chapter 9.
Natural Number 9

Natural Number 9 (NN9)

Natural Number 9 (NN9) holds the container for transformation, bringing the transformation and change processes to completion and releasing the energy to create. Natural Number 9 understands how to include everything, create unity, and shepherd our human experience through the transformation process.

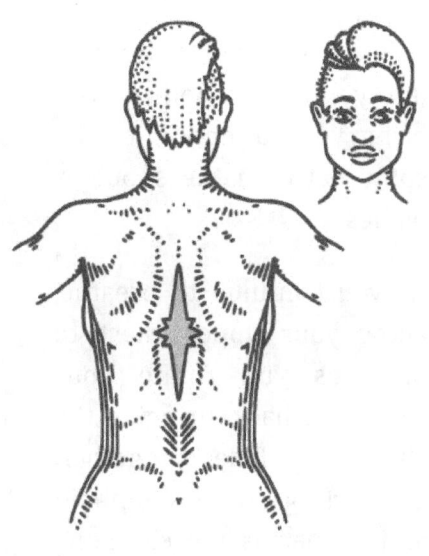

Natural Number 9's Activation Region is along the spine and between the shoulder blades, on the back at the T6/T7 vertebrae, supported by the Rhomboid and lower Trapezius muscles. T7 connects to the lowest rib, which also connects at the bottom of the sternum. This assists with the expansion of the rib cage for breathing. The Trapezius muscles relax at the top where they connect to the shoulders and neck, the Rhomboids pull the shoulder blades back and down, and the Trapezius contracts in along the spine forming a cradle that supports T6/T7 at the spine and balances the body through the back.

People of NN9 know we are all inter-connected. It's as if they see and tailor the fabric of humanity. They are aware of the impact of any force, action, or change within the totality. Because they live with continual awareness, they know that every action we take and every thought we have affects all else around us. Those with this Natural Number know that everything matters, and that nothing matters. They help us process and digest our experiences so that things may come to an end and begin again with a fresh start. First noticing and then pointing out when things are not balanced they invite us to bring ourselves, our community, our world back into equilibrium.

Natural Number 9 Activation Posture

Take a series of deep breaths into your whole body as you bring your attention to the spine between the shoulder blades.

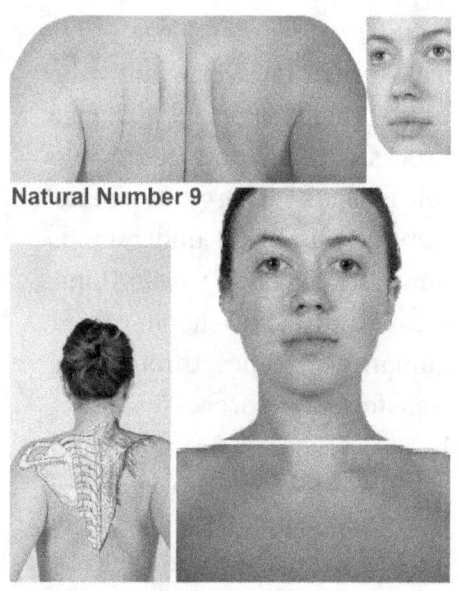

Natural Number 9

As you continue to breathe, allow your upper chest to open as you rotate your shoulders back, bringing the shoulder blades together, contracting the Rhomboid and Trapezius muscle along the spine and relaxing at the top of shoulders.

Keeping your hands open, rotate your palms back, turning them upward, and allow your arms to go back as far as is comfortable in alignment with your breathing; the shoulders will drop down and back as the upper chest expands, and the shoulder blades relax together down the back.

Breathe deeply into your body, allowing your breath to release tension. Move and adjust your body as you release tension and increase mobility.

Core Values for Natural Number 9s:

Flow: NN9s understand that we exist in a flow of energy. Their understanding of our oneness in this flow informs them of how to affect the dynamics of a situation **without using excess energy or force.**

Balance: NN9s value balance in their environments and relationships. They know when things are not balanced, when one side of the scale is tipped in favor of the other. They are always looking for ways to correct the disparity.

Harmony: NN9s want us all to live in harmony, each person taking responsibility for their own actions for a fairer, more inclusive human experience.

Inclusion: NN9s know when someone or something has been actively excluded. They know that, when there is oneness, nothing can be excluded, so they will work to be sure all is included.

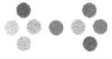

Section 2: Practices for Presence and Creation

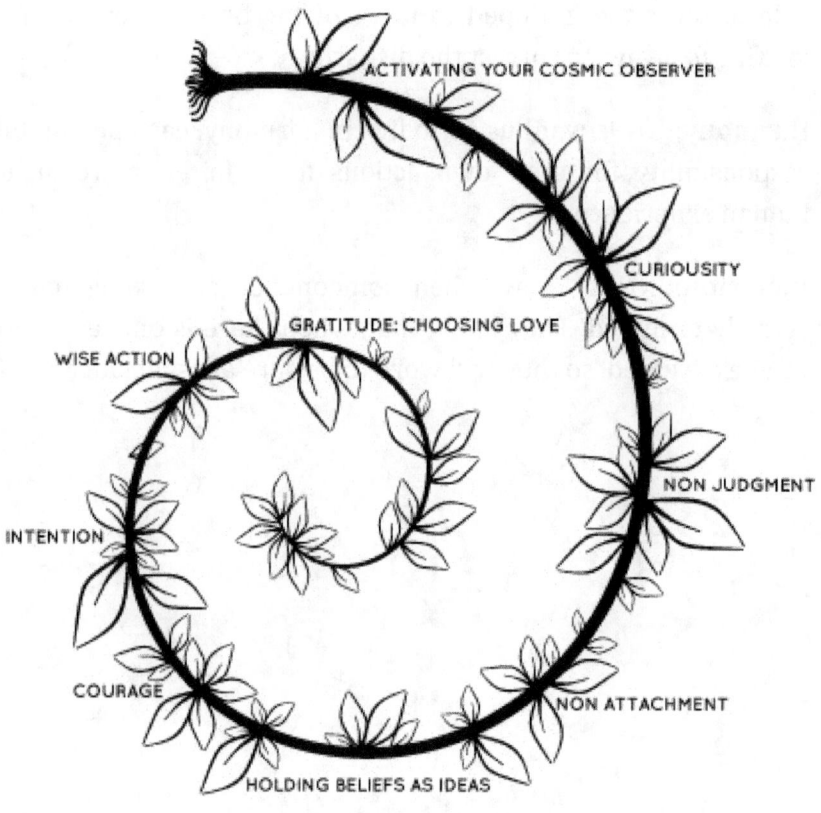

Practices for Presence and Creation

The questions most commonly asked after the first experience of activating a person's Natural Number is "What do I do now that I know? And what is the benefit?" The answer to both questions is at once simple and complex. Identifying your Natural Number starts you on a path toward living your life consciously, on purpose. Even if you do nothing more to practice or bring awareness to your Posture of Activation, a subtle change will begin, and over time you will get happier and feel more fulfilled. If you practice your Activation Posture, learn to activate the other eight postures, and actively follow the Practices for Presence and Creation presented in this section of the book, your transformation will accelerate.

Through the work of learning to understand and describe the Natural Numbers, a deeper understanding of what each Natural Number brings to community has emerged. We have also undergone our own personal transformational process through learning how to activate the Regions of our bodies. We have observed that people will naturally begin to follow the Practices for Presence and Creation outlined here if they: 1) learn to use their body to activate their Natural Number; 2) learn to activate other Natural Numbers in their body; 3) practice activations regularly.

The Practices for Presence and Creation have been understood and taught to Body of 9 by people of each of the Natural Numbers. However, the Practices are not tied specifically to each of the individual Natural Numbers. In fact, each of the Natural Numbers will implement and experience each Practice in a different way.

The benefits of following the Practices are myriad. They assist us with developing and maintaining a positive perspective, even while we heal and grow. The Practices allow our actions to come from a place of conscious alignment with our deepest being; they help us shift our reality to one based on our purpose. In other words, we get to consciously choose how we view and act within a certain set of circumstances. We don't need to descend into fear, surrender to trauma, or allow past experiences—good or bad—to define who we are in the moment. By making the Practices part of our lives, they accelerate us on our path, improve relationships, and alleviate self-imposed suffering, leading to a happier more fulfilling way of life.

Identifying your Natural Number and learning to activate all nine Natural Numbers consciously in the body makes living true to these Practices easier, allowing them to be more easily understood and integrated, becoming habit or second nature.

None of the perspective shifts that stem from the Practices are "easy," yet each one of them is "simple"—that seems to be the way of the universe, doesn't it? Transformation is less complex than we make it out to be. It is a continual commitment to small but significant shifts in perspective that allow us to create happier and more fulfilling realities. You may have heard of all of the Principles presented in this book from various sources. What is unique about our approach, however, is the physical nature of the process, the specific order, and the relationships of the Practices one to another. For those who know their Natural Number, it is also the integration of our physical and spiritual wisdom into the Practice processes.

A commitment to the Practices for Presence strengthens our ability to access and give the power of our Natural Number to others. In turn, the stronger our access to our own Natural Number—and the other eight—the easier it is to be present in the Practices. When you consciously activate your Natural Number through postural adjustment, your awareness expands and you are better able to perceive and respond to the world.

The Practices for Presence and Creation will work for us whether we know our Natural Number or not. And yet, they get easier to perform, and accelerate our transformation, when we know how to activate our Natural Number and use it consciously to increase the awareness of our body's wisdom.

The Practices are interrelated. Each skill reveals and sets the stage for what is possible in the next Practice. There is a progression to the Practices. However, when you are familiar with them all, you will be able to move fluidly back and forth between them in order to activate the skill or Practice needed in the moment to bring you to the present and to move you forward on your path of purpose.

Here is where you begin to learn to connect back to yourself, to peel away the nurture, and get back to the core underlying strength, skills, and natural way of being that comes with your body. Your Natural Number has a tremendous influence on your journey to self-awareness.

It is freeing to: 1) develop an awareness of who you are; 2) understand how your nurtured beliefs systems shape your behaviors; 3) learn how to make conscious choices with the knowledge of your personal physiology – your Natural Number. That is what these sections are designed to help you do.

As you read through, think about the definitions of the words used to describe the practices – what do those words mean to you? How does your interpretation of the words affect how you would approach each section. People of each Natural Number will go about these sections in a particular way, that is different. Integrating your understanding of your Natural Number into this process will make it all the more valuable.

Practices for Presence

These sections provide a series of practices that can be done in order, or in any way that resonates for you. It is important to understand that you will create your own meaning, understanding and version of what is presented here. The stories and examples may or may not resonate for you. Look for the messages in each section that resonate for you.

Chapter 10. Awaken the Observer

Chapter 11. Use Curiosity to Open your Awareness

Chapter 12. Practice Non-Judgment

Chapter 13. Hold Beliefs as Ideas and Possibilities

Chapter 10.
Awaken The Observer

Only when we are able to face ourselves, see where we are, and accept the truth (or un-truth) in what others say about us—and what we say about ourselves—can real change occur. Developing the skill of self-observation, we begin to notice our behaviors, choices, and beliefs, and how they function in our lives. This gives us the information we need to make different and more empowering choices. Learning to activate our Observer is a critical first step to transformation.

The Observer is the soul-level, grander self that knows all and sees all from a neutral perspective. When you activate your Natural Number, there is an immediate shift that creates a sense of calm, ease, joy, and richness in what you perceive and how you respond.

Once again the sensations and way of experiencing life that each of the Natural Numbers feel are completely different, but with each there is a sense of peace and knowing, an ability to perceive what is important to our soul-level being. It initiates our soul to take the lead in our actions.

Natural Number and the Observer

You can activate your Observer at any time. However, it is much easier if you know your Natural Number. This is because each Natural Number offers a simple postural activation described in the chapters on each Natural Number that allows you to switch on your Observer.

The Observer is radically different than the voices or messages we hear/think that continually feed us advice based on our belief systems, life experience, and judgments. These continuous thoughts of the inner critic flow from our entrenched belief systems. They can result in triggered emotional responses, like shame, blame, or fear, which keep us from observing the truth of the present moment. Often these emotional responses are out of alignment with what is really happening.

The Observer remains neutral. It is able to assess the world from our most natural self, our deepest and best place, without applying judgment. It takes in our environment from a spiritual vantage place, sometimes described as a five thousand foot (or big picture) perspective. Each Natural Number will describe the feeling of their Observer with different words. Our Observer allows us to view the current moment as part of a larger narrative, without getting triggered by our deep-seated beliefs.

Through simple postural adjustment, taking a deep breath, and bringing consciousness to your Natural Number Region, if known, or by simply aligning and straightening your body posture if you don't yet know your Natural Number, your body will immediately calm down and make room for the wisdom of the Observer. In this way, you can take in a situation without judgment, and see what is going on in a new way.

How does the Observer Manifest?

Each of us has access to our Cosmic Self through our Natural Number and the Posture of Activation. Depending on your Natural Number, you will have a very different sense of your Cosmic Self. The commonality across the Natural Numbers is that the active Cosmic Self provides access to new information, which is imperceptible *except* when your Natural Number is activated.

For example:
- **Natural Number 1** opens up to a hyperawareness of the beauty of Source that is present all around us. It is a timeless, flowing, infinite place where all is good.

- **Natural Number 2** creates heightened connection to other people, nature, or animals, and through this intense engagement a sense of well-being is created.

- **Natural Number 3** feels joy from connection with the soul, which helps them become an embodied and effortless cheerleader for others.

- **Natural Number 4** builds a deep, innate sensing of what is in alignment, which guides their actions and thoughts.

- **Natural Number 5** experiences the Observer as the sensation of rising above and looking down on the situation from a higher perspective.

- **Natural Number 6** expands the chest to activate their Observer. The chaotic vibration of the world comes into alignment and becomes comprehensible. A sense of peace and heightened awareness— and an excitement about life— replaces the chaos.

- **Natural Number 7**, through focus on the third eye area, creates a still, empty place from where the person can observe without involvement, opening the mind to download new information and see new possibility.

- **Natural Number 8** feels the ease in their body in combination with a sense of both supreme power and gentleness, and standing on solid ground, they are able to feel the rightness in a situation in all the cells of their body.

- **Natural Number 9** opens and expands through the breath, expanding the awareness, allowing the present moment to fit into a much larger picture, creating a sense of fluidity in our interconnection.

Each Natural Number activation creates a calming, expanding, centering experience in which more insight and wisdom become available.

When first beginning to activate our Observer, either through knowing how our posture can support its activation, or by simply paying attention to our breath and sitting up straight, new information will present itself in any given situation. We become calm, expanded, and open, perceiving from a new place, one that is not held captive by our emotions.

Shame, Fear and Disappointment

Shame, fear, and disappointment are triggered in us by our judgments and belief systems. When one or more of these emotions take hold, they pull us out of the present moment, transporting us into the past, often filled with regrets or resentments, or toward a future that we can fear.

Uprooted from the present moment, we can find ourselves in fight-or-flight mode, infused with adrenaline-fueled stress and panic. Our stomachs may churn, our bodies clench, and our minds start attacking us.

As you can imagine, it's very difficult to access your Observer in this state of being! Knowing this, however, is the first step. Here is where we can bring in our postural adjustment and breathing, using your body to awaken your Observer. Your Observer can then provide you with needed information about what is *actually* happening in the present moment, rather than what your judging mind *thinks* is happening.

• • • • • • • • •

Careena's Story: Historical Abandonment and Mistreatment Create Hair-triggers

Careena grew up in poverty, with alcoholism and abuse in the family. Her unstable childhood experiences instilled little sense of safety, love, or caring. In her adulthood she managed to create a beautiful and loving family.

Within her new family she felt the way she had always wanted to feel as a child in her own family: safe and loved. She worked very hard to come to terms with her parents, forgiving and accepting them as she gained an adult perspective. At some level she still hoped to feel some love from them.

It was the day after her fortieth birthday. She was spending it with some close friends. They were talking, and Careena opened up about her deep disappointment that neither parent had called to wish her a "happy birthday." She saw this as further evidence that her parents truly didn't love her, not in the slightest. "It is the final straw. They have never cared about me and never will." She was so angry and hurt that she was having trouble being present to the love around her in that moment.

Ironically, the next day when she checked her voicemail messages, she realized that both of her parents had actually called to wish her happy birthday, but somehow the messages hadn't gotten through. A wall of relief, and a little sense of hope, came over Careena. In a calmer and more centered place, she could appreciate how her friends and husband had held her, and how much of an emotional trigger her parents still held for her. Her Cosmic Self, now active, allowed her to recognize her wholeness, and to see that disappointment is a huge triggering emotion that immediately transports her into her old story.

What does it mean to use the Observer to see our own behaviour?

Learning to see our own behavior requires developing the part of us that can see what we are doing from a neutral place, even as events unfold. The Observer allows us to recognize our own emotional state, despite our current emotional response to a situation.

The Observer in us can take a neutral position, assess what is going on, and inform us of what is really happening. This ability to take stock of ourselves neutrally, even when our emotional state is fully engaged, brings us to a choice; we can shift, diving into our emotions more fully, or take different direction than the one that has us in its thrall in the moment.

Another way to think about this is that we all experience an inner soundtrack, or internal dialogue. Our internal dialogue can take over our actions and become the driver, causing us to give over to the actions of our emotionally triggered state. This is our default position. For example, when someone cuts us off driving and creates a dangerous situation, our fight-or-flight instincts get triggered and we might yell at the other driver, making all sorts of claims that they are an "a**hole" and an idiot. However, in all likelihood, they are a person just like us who happened to encroach on our space in a way that didn't feel safe, triggering fear. When fear takes hold of our being, we lose sight of what really happened. We might become more aggressive than is warranted in the moment, lose control of our self-awareness, and say or do things that we regret once we have calmed down.

Conversely, the internal voice might shut us down, shaming us, and causing us not to speak up when we should have. Careena, in the earlier story, might have turned inward and allowed her internal dialogue to descend into shaming herself, telling herself that she was not lovable. When we lose our awareness and control over our behavior choices, our Observer is unable to work on our behalf as a reasonable overseer.

● ● ● ● ● ● ● ● ●

Susan's Story: Allowing the Observer Time to Kick In

In 2015 we put our California house on the market as a first step to moving to Montana. The process seemed to go on for a very long time, and I repeatedly felt disappointed that we hadn't closed on the house. Each time there was a delay, I would lose my connection to my Observer. Angry, disappointed, and afraid, I fell victim to a whole parade of disturbing emotions.

The first step out of any emotional spiral is to activate your Observer. Notice where you are, what you are saying, inspect the truth, and allow your Observer to name your emotions. If you can take yourself up a level by activating your Observer, then you can begin to shift things to a new perspective.

In the throes of my disappointment, I wrote an email to the person who was putting up roadblocks to the real estate transaction. I was angry and exasperated. A vitriolic diatribe spewed forth from me about their incompetence and lack of care.

After writing—but not sending—this rather biting email, I was clearer about my feelings. My Observer was kicking in, helping me see exactly what was going on for me. In my Natural Number 6, I aligned with my posture of activation by expanding my chest. Suddenly, everything was clearer. As I breathed, continuing to expand my chest, I sensed the truth: no one was incompetent or out to get me.

My emotions stemmed from a deep-seated fear that the transaction would fall through and we would be left in a state of financial panic. Deep in my bones, I felt the importance of this move and was impatient to get going. Every day dragged by like an eternity. I felt as if I was in a prison controlled by our Real Estate guards. From this new realization, I knew an important message needed to be communicated to certain parties. Calmed by my Observer, I could now say what I needed to say, in a manner that could be heard by others.

The Observer can be applied in any circumstance—breathe, expand, and open to yourself. Observe your behavior, notice it, and name the emotions. Try looking below the surface to the deeper reasons for your behavior.

Practicing this in less complex and less triggering situations will begin to build your conscious practices, so you can be open to your Observer's wisdom during tougher challenges. Witnessing yourself is the first step in becoming present enough to change.

● ● ● ● ● ● ● ● ●

Joni's Story: Being Willing to See Our Own Behaviour

Joni woke up with the familiar pit of fear in her stomach. It never seemed to leave her, this fear of financial ruin, fear of losing everything, fear of her ex-husband, fear for her children. Then a smile came to her face as she remembered: today she had volleyball with the ladies—sunshine in the middle of the storm. She looked forward to feeling the sand between her toes, the sun warming her body, and the joy of connection with her volleyball partner.

The volleyball court was the only place where she still felt her personal power and the pleasure of moving in her body. She loved the flow of the perfect pass, the perfect set, the full satisfaction of pounding a volleyball into the sand, or making the perfect cut-shot to send her opponent diving fruitlessly for the ball. "Today will be a good day," she thought to herself.

As she mused on the upcoming game, the phone rang. It was her volleyball partner. The words that came next stung more than any pounding hit. "Joni, I've tried so hard to be your friend, but I just can't do it anymore. You are so negative—so down—that being around you is too difficult. I wanted to tell you that we won't be inviting you back to play volleyball with us." The only light in Joni's long tunnel went dark.

Joni's once gregarious, positive, fun-loving self was now so lost that people were actively choosing not to be around her. No wonder she felt desperately alone.

Joni knew she had to take a closer look at her negative behavior.

Almost every thought began with, "Joe did this to me. Joe is an ass... Why won't Joe take responsibility?" She was filled with so much bitterness, she realized that she didn't even like being with herself. She called the one friend who seemed willing to be with her no matter where she was.

"Jane, can you help me? I want to stop saying negative things about my ex-husband. In fact, I want to stop saying negative things, period."

"Well it's about time!" Jane replied. "You have my full support."

That one call from her volleyball partner shocked Joni sufficiently to see just how often she allowed negativity to dominate her thoughts and actions. Being able to step back and observe herself allowed Joni to see what had happened, and opened doors for change—for a different possibility. If Joni had understood how to activate her Observer by activating her Natural Number, she might have gotten herself out of her negative spiral much more quickly and without the trauma. But anything that interrupts the flow of our habitual, negative inner talk opens us up to the potential for listening to a deeper and more enduring wisdom.

● ● ● ● ● ● ● ● ●

Ralph's Story: Observation Allowed Me to Find a Way Back to Myself

Things for Ralph were tough financially. He had lost his job and the financial demands of keeping a family together were an increasing strain on him. His anxiety and fear mounted as his savings slipped away and mountains of credit card debt loomed, threatening to block any possibility of an end in sight.

Ralph needed his credit card company to cut him some slack while he sold a property. He called the credit card company to ask for help, even though this made him very uncomfortable.

A foreign-sounding person answered his call, sounding brusque, as if he was already having a bad day. In response, Ralph's knee-jerk judgments kicked-in and his anxiety skyrocketed. "This guy doesn't even speak English; how will he be able to help me? I can already tell he doesn't care about me." Stressful thoughts filled Ralph's mind. As Ralph explained his situation to the representative, he imagined the negativity flowing toward him through the phone. "I'm sorry sir, we are unable to help you. And your available credit—we'll need to lower that too. Your credit risk has been raised by our analysts."

Ralph's anxiety and shame stormed through him, an internal roar. He was about to blow up with outrage and disappointment. *I'm a long-time customer*, he thought. *I only need a two-week extension.* He almost yelled the words at the customer service rep: "Why won't you help me?"

Then he took a deep breath, opened his throat—as he had learned to do when his Natural Number 1 was identified—and he felt himself calm down. His Observer kicked in, and gentle sense of vulnerability filled his being.

Connected now to a sensation of well-being and beauty, his habitual path of yelling at the customer service representatives fell away. "Wow, I can truly understand how your organization needs to take this stance. It must be very tough having to tell people in need that you can't help them. Is there another possibility here that we haven't explored as a way of protecting your organization and still assisting me?"

The customer service rep's response was remarkable: "Let me talk with my supervisor to see if there is another way." Ralph was put on hold for a few minutes and when the rep returned, he had a solution. "Sir, you have a little credit left on your other card with us. We could transfer that credit to this card to tide you over, avoiding fees and keeping your credit intact."

Ralph realized how much he needed his Observer when going into these types of interactions. He also realized that he needed to take care of his body. If he was hungry, or tired, or in a state of fear or resentment when he started a call, he could be sure it wasn't going to go well. Over time, by using his Observer and adjusting his posture, he would notice when his emotions would start to trigger, and he could begin to adjust before things got out of hand. His Observer was opening new avenues for behavior choices that were resulting in more fulfilling outcomes.

Exercises for Self Observation:

Your Strongest Emotions Are Your Greatest Teachers. We recommend that you create a workbook for the exercises in this book. Your answers build upon the work that you do in each chapter. Find a notebook or journal to use as your workbook for your Practices. Answer the following questions in your workbook:

1. Look back over the course of the last week or month. Can you remember any instances where you had an emotional response that was bigger or smaller than the situation might have warranted, or that surprised you in some way? Did your response feel out of alignment or out of proportion with the situation? List as many of these examples as you can recall, without judging yourself for them.

2. Look at your examples. Do you recognize a common trigger or pattern? Is there something consistent that underlies these emotional responses? For example, does looking in a mirror cause you to criticize yourself?

3. Pick one of the examples and reflect on how you dealt with the situation. Were you aware of your behavior in the moment? Did you notice the impact you were having on any other people present? What kind of emotional response did you get back from the other person/people?

4. If you had been more aware, could you have chosen a different response? Write down other approaches to try in the future. Is there one thing you wish you had done or said differently?

5. For the next week or so, remind yourself to pay attention when you find yourself in a similar situation. Stop, take a deep breath, stand or sit straight and, if you know how, consciously activate your Natural Number through your postural alignment. Allow your Observer to kick in. Pay attention to your behavior, as you may quickly get re-triggered. That's ok. If you get too triggered for your Observer to help you, exit the situation as gracefully as you can, and try again when you are calm.

6. Note the behavior of people with whom you are interacting when your Observer is active and when it is not. Can you see a difference?

Your Toughest Interactions are also your Greatest Teachers.
Answer the following question in your workbook:

1. Look back on the interactions that you had with people over the last week. Did they appear to be happy with you, and interested in your conversation? Did you notice if they were engaged with what you were talking about? Were they trying to make eye contact with you, or looking away?

2. If they were not engaged, and it felt like they wanted to leave the conversation, is it possible that your actions or words were responsible? Do you remember what you were talking about? Was your Observer engaged at that moment?

3. If you were trying to resolve a conflict, or have your point of view heard, did you feel as if they were listening to you? Were you listening to them? Think back on your emotional state: were you happy, irritated, upset, or afraid? What did you do in response to your emotions?

4. If you had engaged your Observer, what might you have changed about your behavior and your interaction?

If you are upset about something and can't get your head to stop spinning around it—and you are not able to activate your Observer—what should you do?

If adjusting your posture and breathing into your Natural Number doesn't work to bring you more present, and you need to vent, one technique is to allow yourself to rant in an email that you never send, or write your stream of consciousness in a journal. This allows you to give voice to your emotions without dumping them on others.

Be aware that you may temporarily move deeper into the uncomfortable feelings. Be sure that you have adequate time to work all the way through your process. This gives your Observer a chance to kick in.

After you have written everything you want, take a deep breath, adjust your physical posture, and allow your Observer to activate.

What do you notice in what you've written? Can you see where your response is out of alignment with the situation?

Look deeper into your triggers or rise above to a different perspective. As you become more curious about your behavior, through your ability to observe yourself in action, you are setting the groundwork for the next step in the Practices.

You can come back and read this chapter again, or review your answers in your workbook, and apply them to a current situation. You can also come back and apply the skill of curiosity—described next—to any situation, past or present.

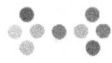

Chapter 11.

Use Curiosity to Open Awareness

Exercising curiosity invites openness and exploration. Being curious means looking for new information, different possibilities, or a deeper understanding of what we already have experienced, and what is just now showing up. It means staying open to new information, perspectives, and ways of being that would be inaccessible to us without getting curious.

Curiosity can work like a giant broom, clearing out the clutter of old thoughts that keep us from taking in new information. Curiosity transforms outmoded thought patterns into powerful questions and deep explorations. Rather than saying to ourselves, "Oh, I already know this, nothing new here," we can listen to what another person has to say. We infuse our thinking with a spirit of inquiry: "Wow, what do they really mean? What makes them hold this particular perspective? What is true here for this person?" Thus, we learn how to pay attention. We invite others to openly share with us, and ultimately become increasingly curious about them as well. Activating your Observer allows you to be curious and present simultaneously.

Remember there are nine totally different kinds of people, each with their own life experiences. They have a gift to share with you. Curiosity opens you to receiving their gifts.

How Do You Exercise Curiosity?

Curiosity is about the beginner's mind. Rather than half listening to someone, while actually scanning our own experience to see if we already know what's being said, we attune our whole being to the other person.

If we start every interaction, every experience, every study or learning with the idea that we don't have all the answers, then we open up to being surprised and transformed by new information. Taking it a step further, by receiving information without having to embed it in a familiar context or category—as in: "Is it like (X thing you are familiar with)?"—we enter a position to expand our consciousness and experience base.

While making connections between different information and ideas can be helpful, starting with a blank slate allows us to be present to a new thought *before* integrating it. Curiosity leads to creativity, which is sparked when our curiosity is piqued and we start to explore. Creativity is the process of pulling together the known, the unknown, the possible, and the as yet impossible, to birth something new into the world. Curiosity is key to newness.

Adding Wonder and Awe to Enhance Curiosity:

Wonder and awe are emotions that we might have experienced more often as a child; maybe we wondered how Santa delivered all those presents to all the kids in the world in one night. We are talking about the feeling of wonderment at the manifestation of something incredible.

Awe is the feeling we get when we deeply appreciate the beauty or majesty of something. This most commonly happens when we experience nature: a sunset, a beautiful landscape, the perfection of a flower. We feel awe at the incredible creative power contained within what we are experiencing.

Curiosity is a skill we can all develop. When we add wonder and awe to the mix, we discover the playful and joyful aspect of entering new experiences, freed from our own agendas. The lens of wonder puts us back in a childlike state of awareness, bringing the "WOW!" factor back into our perceptions. Wonder quiets the voices that work hard to keep us secure by keeping us from change. Awe opens us to the beauty and creative power of what we are experiencing. Awe-inspiring moments are available to us at any time. Awe helps us to perceive natural beauty and the sacredness of any moment.

● ● ● ● ● ● ● ● ●

Ashley: On Remembering Curiosity

When Ashley, a person with Natural Number 4, was in elementary school, she wondered at the magical aspects of nature. Exploring the world around her, she would be overcome with excitement at the smallest thing: a hornet's nest, a parade of ants, the smile on her best friend's face. She remembers feeling such freedom and joy as she rushed around the playground from one wonder to another.

One time, she and a friend got curious about what would happen if they created their own ant's nest. They got a large jar, filled it with sand and then with ants. They spent a whole day totally absorbed by the ant's activities, feeling nothing but joy and curiosity as they observed and learned. Later that day, they excitedly showed the jar of ants to their big sister, who had Natural Number 8. "We are going to fill it with water to see if they can swim!" Ashley exclaimed.

Her sister was appalled and upset that they would torture the ants in this way; every cell of her body responded, as if to an emergency.

"Ashley, how could you be so beastly? You will kill them all if you flood that jar." The older sister shamed them, really without meaning to, into stopping. For the girls, it felt like she took all the joy out of the experiment. They freed the ants and went off to watch television with their tails between their legs, feeling as if they had done something really horrible.

Here in this story you see how the different perspectives of the Natural Numbers interpret and hold different values around the same experiences, how shame can be used to shut down people's curiosity and joy, even in the most innocent of circumstances. Ashley's curiosity was not supported by her sister. Her sister didn't see it as curiosity and allowed her emotional response to shame and frighten Ashley, shutting down her curiosity to explore. Handled differently, Ashley might have freed the ants while keeping her curiosity intact.

Shame, fear, and disappointment can close down our access to curiosity, wonder, and awe. When we are shamed—by ourselves or others—we become afraid to repeat behaviors that might cause us to feel that shame again. When we become disappointed with the outcomes of our explorations, we become less willing to try new things. If our curiosity isn't strong enough to overcome our shames, fears, and disappointments, we stop learning, stop trying new things, and constrain our behaviors. Before long, we find ourselves stuck in a rut, settled and secure in our "safe" place.

When we are young, for example, playing sports can be a way to revel in the power of our bodies and the joy of physical connection. It is not until sports become competitive, a battle of abilities and mind-games aimed at defeating our rivals, that shame, fear, and disappointment creep in.

If you watch 4-year-old children playing soccer, you can see that they just don't care about who wins, who scores a goal, and how they look out on the field. They are simply relishing running around, chasing a ball, and having fun with their bodies. Many of us lose this innocence, this connection to our bodies, and the wisdom they hold for us, **especially** when sports become a cutthroat activity where we are judged as "good" or "weak." Pressure to perform, fear of disappointing others, and striving to be a winner—at all costs—has a high price, as you will see as we continue with Ashley's story.

Ashley: Closing Down through Competition

As Ashley entered junior high and high school, trying to fit in, compete, and perform squeezed the joy out of her life. Everything became a competition, where the importance of winning became paramount. She joined the tennis team and made number three as a freshman; everyone was so "proud" of her. One day she was playing against the toughest school in the division and was losing her match.

Her coach came over to her and said angrily, "What are you doing Ashley? Stop trying to play her game and get the ball over the net and in the court. I've never seen you play worse. Where is your head?" It felt like she had been punched in the stomach.

Up to that point she thought she had been holding her own and playing pretty well against a far stronger and more experienced athlete. Her coach's judgmental and negative attitude stole her confidence, her joy, and her willingness to remain open to ways in which she could play better tennis. His words shut her down. The joy of the physical experience of running after a ball, hitting a clean shot, and trying new things with her body left her. She was afraid and frozen. The curiosity, wonder, and awe that had imbued her with a love of tennis were gone.

John: Wondering Why he went to College

John lost his academic curiosity in high school and became a memorizing machine. He regurgitated facts to please teachers and parents, while critical thinking, curiosity, and exploration became close to impossible—they took too much time away from "getting things done." Fear of not succeeding froze his creativity, and closed the door on his love of learning.

Life in college served up mixed messages. Some teachers encouraged him to find his way back to curiosity. Others followed in the model of high school, piling on the work to see who would rise above the rest. But one professor instilled hope. He asked John to answer the question, "What is the purpose of ___?" and to fill in the blank with whatever was calling to him at that time.

As he was in the process of graduating, John naturally asked himself, "What was the purpose of my college education?" At first, it all felt rather pointless. But the question began to stimulate that old sense of curiosity, wonder, and awe for learning that he recalled from when he was a very young child. He began to see his experience at college in a new light. He realized that he actually loved learning, exploring, and seeking. He found his connection back to curiosity, reconnected with the joy of wonder, awe, and newfound possibilities.

Exercises for Curiosity:

Learning from your Past:

Review your experiences and pick one where someone started to tell you about something you hadn't heard about before. Reflect back: what was your first reaction?

Write down in your workbook what you thought about the person, what they were telling you, and what you were thinking as they spoke to you. Be honest with yourself; no one else need ever know. What did you say in response?

What do you notice about your recollection? Return to the exact same experience, but this time with your curiosity on high alert. Reflect back: did you tell yourself that you already knew what they were saying, or think it was uninteresting, or that they were repeating themselves?

Why do you think they wanted to impart this information to you? Did you make some kind of judgment about what they were saying? How did you hold what they were saying?

Could you have been more curious, or introduced wonder and awe as they were telling you about this experience? If you had, what might have happened?

Exercise in Curiosity, Wonder, and Awe:

Find someone with whom to enter into a conversation. It could be at a party, a work meeting, or with a friend at lunch. Choose your time, place, and person. For a period of time, only ask questions about what they are telling you, such as, "Why…? How did you feel…? What was important to you…?"

If you notice that you begin to make up your mind about how you feel about what they are telling you, try saying, "Wow—that's really cool! What else can you tell me?"

Keep the questions going, and listen to the answers. Each answer will give rise to new questions. With each revelation or answer, marvel at how interesting this information is. It may feel very strange and childlike at first, but stay with it. When you get home, journal in your workbook about the experience.

Chapter 12.
Practice Non-Judgment

Holding a perspective of non-judgment is another way to remain open to new information or a fresh perspective. By non-judgment, I mean not placing yourself, what you know, or what you believe above or below anything or anyone else. Judgment is the voice in your head that says things like, "Can you believe that person just did ..." or, "You're so stupid! I can't believe you just did that." It is the voice that makes you feel better or worse about yourself than somebody else. It is the voice that is indignant, incredulous, and critical; that puts you or someone else up or down.

Say you meet a friend for lunch, and she looks great. You feel tired and frumpy and showed up in jeans and a sweatshirt. If you begin to internally criticize yourself—or your friend—for the difference in how you look, you will never be present to the moment. When you tell yourself, "Oh wow, she looks great and I am a total slob," we see a simple example of how we constantly evaluate ourselves as superior or inferior to others. The act of thinking these competitive and comparative thoughts takes you out of what is actually happening. Rather than just greeting your friend, connecting with her, and taking her in at a deeper level, you are stuck in a comparison that immediately creates a sense of disconnection and separation.

Our Western culture values success, and it trains us to compare and evaluate where we land in terms of *everything*: work, relationships, appearances, possessions, and home. Every magazine we pick up reinforces the message of comparison and competition. We are trained to measure ourselves as part of a hierarchy of winners and losers. Where do we fit into the pecking order? How do we stack up?

Notice how often throughout the day a thought similar to this one crosses your mind: "Am I ... enough?" This question can result in a sense of lacking that closes us off from the acceptance of "what is." Acceptance without judgment is a requirement for transformation. When we accept ourselves as we are, and accept the circumstances and the people around us—just as *they* are—then we are ready to evolve and transform on the spiritual path.

When stuck in an endless cycle of comparison, satisfaction comes from winning, being more than someone, or having more of something. The flip side is losing, or being less. Neither is in service of our highest good. Notice when we judge, then thank our judge (don't make the judge wrong because that's just more judging!), then let go of the judgment and see what else is there.

Defensiveness is a Response to Perceived Judgment

When we feel judged, it's a common response to be defensive. When we respond defensively, it's a cue that it is time to activate our Observer and look at what entrenched belief has been questioned or challenged. Defensiveness is usually in response to an internal judgment. For example, if someone makes a comment about your driving, how do you respond? If you respond defensively, you might want to look at the underlying reasons for your response; it is a great clue to the self-judgment that you are generating in response to the comment.

• • • • • • • • •

Susan's Story: Learning to Observe our Judge

I was first introduced to the concept of Non-Judgment when I attended a workshop in my early forties. The group was asked to follow a couple of simple guidelines: 1) Exercise non-judgment; 2) only speak or act in-service of the group. We were stunned by these requests, realizing that literally everything we planned to say included judgment and was primarily in service of ourselves. For two days we remained almost silent as we began to witness our behavior and quiet our internal judge. This was extraordinarily hard for everyone. It brought to light all kinds of drama and aspects of our behavior that were utterly eye opening and at times jaw dropping.

One participant freaked out so badly that he began verbally attacking the leaders. He was in so much discomfort that he could not witness himself and disengage from the cycle of judgment. It was as if a dark cloud had descended over him and taken control of his otherwise gentle soul.

The exercise was powerful, but it was incomplete. If we stop judging or proving, what do we do instead? How do we keep ourselves from reverting to old habits? That's where the power of the nine Natural Numbers comes in. When we are reminded to use our physical posture and activation to bring ourselves back to presence and the present, we are given a tool that we can access at any time, in order to break the cycle of anger, shame, and judgment.

For example, if I find myself being defensive, or needing to have the last word, I expand my chest and take a deep breath. In this posture, with my Natural Number 6 activated, I look inside again. What is really going on? What is it that I really want to happen in this situation?

This work, quite frankly, is not for the faint of heart. It can take you deep into your demons, and it will change your relationships forever. The young man left the workshop believing he had permanently damaged relationships. Try as he might, he could not release his judgment of himself and the workshop leaders. The truth is that while he had been instructed not to judge, no one had shown him how to detach sufficiently from his judgment to see it clearly for what it was. He had no idea how to activate his own innate body wisdom to help him separate from his old stories and deep wounds.

Each of the Natural Numbers has its own proclivity or style of judgment. These stem from the combination of our experiences and our unconscious Natural Number. If we operate from the assumption that we are all basically the same, we will be greatly confused by the behavior of others. At least eight-ninths of the population doesn't care about the same things that we do. This is a recipe for misunderstanding and chaos at best, fear and loathing at worst.

For example, a person of Natural Number 2 is built for relationship and connection. They care so deeply about relating to others that it would be a rare occurrence for them to put a project or task ahead of a relationship. Always aware of the importance of the person involved in an interaction, they are keen to honor that relationship in every way they can.

But as a Natural Number 6, I tend to focus on moving processes forward and creating the new. Thus, I possess a natural sense of urgency to keep things moving that is part of the drive of Natural Number 6.

I was once driving with a Natural Number 2; I changed lanes and passed another car relatively quickly because I didn't like the speed it was going. I expressed my irritation and my friend quickly reminded me, "Susan, that is not just a car. There is a person driving the car. You might have taken into account that person and their needs."

Honestly, in that moment I realized that I never really considered that other cars were actually the people driving the cars. As a Natural Number 6, I drive in response to the energy of what is around me and focus on getting from point A to point B in the most expeditious manner. I can feel and anticipate what is happening around me; I rarely consciously expand my awareness to think about the person driving the other car.

But my Natural Number 2 friend always considered the person driving the other car. This shows two profoundly different ways to approach driving, neither better than the other—just very different ways of being.

How many times have you stood and listened to a friend expound on all of the wrongs that someone did, or about the terrible and inexcusable behavior of said person? When it is someone else talking, it can be a lot easier to see that there are so many other possible motivations and reasons for what happened.

When we get lost in the tales of our own judges, however, it is way too simple to jump to conclusions and make assumptions about others using only our own yardstick as a measure. Our internal judge, driven by beliefs and fueled by shame, fear, and disappointment, fabricates all kinds of mournful stories that sound real to ours ears, and all too frequently drown out the wider, more forgiving and more helpful perspective.

If we notice that "our story" has taken over, then we know that our judge is ruling the show. Once again we can, by activating our Observer through postural adjustment, quiet the mind chatter, and then make a conscious choice to act a different way.

● ● ● ● ● ● ● ● ●

Joni's Story: Releasing Long-held Judgments to Create Freedom

Joni looked in the mirror, just like she did every day, turned sideways, and examined how fat her stomach looked. Was it going to be a good self-image day, or a day where she berated herself for not being thin enough to have value as a person? She thought back to a time forty years earlier when her then high school boyfriend had first pointed out that she went through this same performance every time she looked in a mirror. Back then, at age sixteen, she weighed one hundred and fifteen pounds. Thin as she was, her inner critic and judge still told her that her stomach wasn't flat enough.

Joni's was just eight years old when she first became aware of self-shaming judgments. She persuaded her mother to buy her a baby-doll bathing suit that covered her small stomach bulge. In high school, she read *Sixteen Magazine,* all the while wishing she could look like the models in the magazine. If she were more beautiful, thinner, then she too would be worthy of love and attention.

During her sophomore year of college, sitting around with a group of senior guys as they made fun of the women who had gained fifteen to twenty pounds, she remembered how self-conscious she felt. As her own body developed, her shame in the changes she was experiencing was so great that she began to binge eat in response. Later still, she would become a distance athlete, dropping thirty pounds until she was just skin and bone. Still, self-esteem eluded her. In the back of her mind she believed that she could lose this battle with self-control at any moment. She felt like a fraud.

Today, at fifty-five years old, and happily married to a man who thinks she is beautiful just the way she is, her self-judgment still stalks her. "How do I change this?" Joni thinks to herself. "How did I ever come to believe that my weight decides my worthiness?" Joni will need to get curious about her underlying beliefs about her body as a first step to loving herself unconditionally, no matter what her weight, or the size of her stomach.

Exercises for Non-Judgment:

It takes a great deal of self-awareness and honesty to notice your own internal judge and admit to seeing the impact it has on your life. And yet, as with any journey, it begins with one small step.

Think of an area where you are prone to putting yourself down, actively criticizing yourself, or glorifying someone else. Notice your internal dialogue. If you hear yourself shaming, criticizing, or expressing despair at an outcome, your judge is likely active. Simple examples might include, "Oh, that was really stupid… I'm a dummy… I look so fat in that… what were you thinking…?"

Make a note of when you judge yourself better or lesser than someone else. "Wow, she has a problem, glad I don't have that," or, "that guy is so ugly," or, "I wish I was as smart as she is." You get the idea—these thoughts are always about comparing yourself to others.

Now it's time to take action.

1. Carry your workbook with you. If you notice yourself placing yourself above or below someone else, write down the thought, and make a tally mark each time you have this same type of thought. For example, if you notice that you, like Joni in the earlier story, have a habit of looking in the mirror and looking for all your faults, then write down, "criticized my body," and each time you catch yourself criticizing your body, make a tally mark. You can keep it as simple as "judged myself" or as detailed as "I told myself I am fat." The objective of this exercise is to begin to notice how much judgment comes into play, and how it shows up in your life.

Another example: You are waiting in line at the grocery store. There is a long line, and the clerk is moving very slowly. You notice yourself becoming irritated with the clerk. Your voices might start by saying, "This guy is so incompetent. Doesn't he realize that all these people are waiting for him? He isn't paying any attention or even trying to be more efficient." That would be three tally marks for judging thoughts.

2. Look at the line of reasoning in your judgments; get curious about the underlying belief. What do you believe that is causing you to make these judgments? It might be that you believe that these things are true about yourself, so when you see them in others it triggers feelings of not being competent and valuable. By noticing your judgments, and looking at the trends more closely, you begin to notice your underlying, deep-seated beliefs.

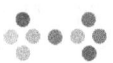

Chapter 13.
Hold Beliefs as Ideas and Possibilities

Our belief systems are incredibly important and have a huge—and often unconscious—effect on how we behave. We develop our belief systems from our life experiences. Something happens, and we decide what it means to us. This story from our experiences becomes a deep-seated belief that we may not even be aware that we have. Being unaware of our deep-seated beliefs can be detrimental to us. When not held consciously, a belief can cause us to behave or respond in ways that make no sense to ourselves or to others. Unless we can understand the underlying belief systems that are driving our behavior, nothing can change.

Belief systems come from our experiences, and include what and how we are taught. The actions, framework, and moral structure of our educational system, as well as our parents', authority figures', and society's conventions in general are built on commonly held belief systems. Learning to recognize these systems, understand their impact and notice how they affect our behavior is a critical part of enabling change.

When beliefs become set in stone, and we place those stones into our spiritual backpack to carry around with us, our attachment to those beliefs can keep us weighed down and held back. It is therefore incredibly freeing to realize that our beliefs are, in fact, fluid, changeable, and adaptable. They aren't set in stone, and we have the power to change them by looking at the bedrock on which they've been built. How do they serve us? How can we set them aside?

The truth is that most of us carry around so many unexamined beliefs that our spiritual backpack is too full to take on new information. The more attached we are to our beliefs, the harder we hold onto them, dragging ourselves down. But if we hold our beliefs lightly, as ideas and possibilities, we can release them when more pertinent or meaningful information is presented[6]. After all, ideas feel much easier to change or set aside.

If you add in the nine different ways that we can perceive the very same experience through understanding the nine Natural Numbers, we start to see how incredibly important it is to be conscious and neutral in our observations, openly aware of how our beliefs drive our behaviors. There is no "one way" to look at anything. There are lots of ways. And that understanding alone adds a quality of dynamism and vitality to the adventure of life.

The invitation here is to see that our personal beliefs, combined with our community, societal, and global beliefs can create the conditions for confusion, pain and suffering. When we run the behaviors and actions of others through a rigid belief system, we are bound to misunderstand, misinterpret, and create a road of reality that is flawed at best. Assuming we know the motivation for other people's behavior, when we ourselves only have a small part of the picture, is fraught with pitfalls, misinterpretation, and misunderstanding. With all of our deep-seated beliefs and judgments, it is a wonder that we ever reach peace and love with each other.

One of the greatest sources of self-imposed suffering is when our internal judge, working in cahoots with our belief system, trips us up. We create a set of realities from our experiences that are diametrically opposed to other realities. We believe that our perspective is "right" and others' perspectives are "wrong." This is a slippery slope that leads to the collision of opposing forces, conflict, and destruction.

---

[6] I want to give credit here to Neil Kramer and his book *The Unfoldment* for introducing the concept of holding beliefs as ideas.

How often do we find ourselves judging and thereby separating ourselves from others based on deep-seated belief systems? Religion is one example where we can congregate around the concept that there is only one path to God—and it's ours. We know that this kind of rigid thinking exists in all kinds of ways and places, whether it is the Western Industrial World proclaiming that capitalism is the only way to go, or someone telling you that their sports team is better than anyone else's, or that people should only eat certain kinds of food. These kinds of deep-seated beliefs allow those who hold them to feel like they belong to a community. But they separate us, too, from anyone who does not share our same beliefs. Our deep-seated beliefs have us misinterpret all kinds of people and situations, and keep us from being present to what is really going on.

When someone we care about does not share our beliefs, it makes us uncomfortable. That's because we attribute value to others based on their professed beliefs, relative to ours. So when another person does not align with our position, we often make erroneous assumptions about the reasons for their actions, and interpret what we think it says about their values. We can't possibly like so and so anymore, because they said or believe xyz.

Just go on Facebook if you want confirmation. Look at any issue out there today and you'll see there are multiple perspectives, each fueled by deeply held beliefs. While this helps us to gather in small online tribes where we find our "folks" and garner lots of "likes," this kind of superficial sharing is also a cause of suffering and dissent.

You can see and read of the hurt and anger that pervades the e-waves, because the actual system is set up to have people agree or disagree, instead of becoming curious about each other, or where our beliefs are actually coming from.

So what do we do about this? One thing is that we can learn to hold our belief systems as ideas and possibilities, keeping the door open for other perspectives and ways of being that can add to the picture, fill out the information, and create greater understanding between all people. We are formed by our belief systems. We operate from them. Our emotions arise from them. They control most aspects of our reality. Given this, isn't it essential that we examine them to be sure that we still want to hold them; that they serve us and guide us to achieve our purpose in the world?

Fortunately, your Observer can examine your beliefs from a neutral place. Once you can look at your beliefs, you can see how they affect your behavior. Then you can choose how you want to hold that belief moving forward.

If we choose to look at our beliefs as ideas and possibilities, they lose their grip and significance, thereby releasing their hold on our emotions and behaviors.

For example, if one chooses to believe in God, but stays open to the possibility that God comes in many forms, and through many words with many associated beliefs, the emotional charge that underlies the belief no longer controls our behavior. We are free to examine and make a conscious decision about the belief—is it still true for me? Is it serving me and the world around me? How strongly do I wish to hold this belief?

Let's circle back to Joni's belief; it can be summed up as "my value is related to my appearance;" thin equals valuable. If you turn that belief upside down, you get different behavior and feelings. My mother was just diagnosed with an illness that could starve her to death if left untreated. It took six months to diagnose the problem. She lost seventeen pounds. If she had not had seventeen pounds to lose, other complications would have ensued. So we could change a belief about weight to something like this: it is important to have some level of fat reserves as we age in order to withstand certain diseases.

Choice creates power and releases us from suffering. By raising our awareness through our Observer, we have the opportunity to release ourselves from self-imposed misery. The process is challenging, and will hit all of our "hot buttons," sending us spiraling off into all kinds of directions. But if you stay with yourself, you will begin to build new, consciously chosen belief systems that you can hold loosely in order to create the conscious reality of your choosing.

In researching the Natural Numbers, my husband, Martin, and I hear stories of what it means to live in the body of each of the Natural Numbers. From this, we construct a picture for people to begin to understand themselves and others. We continually check in with ourselves about anything we begin to hold as belief in this process.

It is impossible not to believe. We at Body of 9 truly believe that there are nine types of human beings, that the nine Natural Numbers and our process for identifying them are true and accurate. Every day we seek to challenge ourselves, continually examining the words we use, the way that we hold our beliefs, and how we put them into action. If our beliefs calcify, we know that we have stopped learning.

● ● ● ● ● ● ● ● ●

Susan's Story: The Impact

Holding beliefs as ideas has been incredibly freeing for me. It helps me see how I mold my sense of the world through experience, and how the interpretation and decisions that I make about those experiences shape my world.

To stay open to change, I pay attention to my attachment response to experiences. If I find myself having an intense attachment in a situation, I again look deeper. What belief am I holding that I can examine as an idea? What shift do I need to make?

A couple of years ago, I identified a person as having Natural Number 5. If you're not familiar with the identifying process, it is a bit like watching a dance, with the identifier—in this case me—physically feeling into the physicality of the person being identified. After this particular session, I received comments back from the person with Natural Number 5 via a mutual friend; they were skeptical about the physical process we use to identify the Natural Numbers. They wondered if I had introduced a personal bias into the way I push on people differently, depending on their energy identification.

My first response was defensive. They didn't get to see others experiencing the process, so what did they know? And yet, as I became more curious and less attached, I realized that it could look that way; in fact, it could be that way. I realized that I must continually hold a neutral and honoring space as I work with people, and be aware of my beliefs and attachments and how they shape my actions in the identification process.

The moment I begin to try to convince someone, I have to look and see if my ego is attached to a belief about being right. This is always the trickiest and slipperiest slope. When my belief attachment involves my own self-worth, it is really hard to stay open. Paying attention to how I hold my beliefs makes it much easier to self-evaluate and re-examine. Then I can take in new information.

• • • • • • • • •

Michael: How Our Deep-seated Beliefs Keep Us Separate

Michael was the youngest of a big family. His parents had, on the one hand, been very strict; on the other, they were too busy to really pay much attention. He did well enough in school that they let him do his own thing. Like other guys his age, he played a lot of video games, and smoked some weed from time to time. One day his dad came home early and caught him smoking with friends in the backyard. He yelled, "I don't ever want to see you depraved kids at my house again! I am going to call your parents and let them know what happened here."

He called all their parents, and of course everyone got in all kinds of trouble. Michael, furious with his dad, yelled at him, called him names, and punched him. His dad took out his belt and began to whip him with it.

"Go to your room," his dad commanded. Michael, reeling from the beating, went to his room, packed a bag, and snuck out of the house. It was a cold winter night. All his friends were in trouble so he had nowhere to go. He tried to find a warm place for shelter. As he calmed down, he began to see the experience from his Dad's side. He decided to go home and see if he could patch things up. When he returned home the door was bolted from inside and his parents wouldn't answer. He slept that night on the porch in the snow.

Now, as he looks back on that experience, he can see how his own behavior escalated the situation. But mostly he is still angry with his dad for his antiquated views and his overbearing and violent response. There are different ways to deal with situations. His father had no ability to stand back and observe his own behavior. Guided by deep-seated beliefs that no longer applied, at least in Michael's reality, his father's fear and judgment overcame his ability to act rationally or compassionately.

Reflecting back on that night, Michael realized that if they had both been aware of their Observers, and had been able to activate them in the moment, they might have been able to move out of their entrenched positions, but neither were equipped to do so. At some level their relationship never fully recovered from the pain of that experience.

Exercises for Deep Seated Beliefs:

Go back to your list of judgments with tally marks that you developed for the chapter on Judgment. Look at the one with the most tally marks. Activate your Observer, then ask yourself the following:

1. What is the deeper underlying belief? Keep peeling the onion until you can express it as simply as possible.

2. Is there another underlying belief below the one you just voiced? Dig until the core belief is uncovered.

3. Ask yourself if this core belief is something that you want to hold, or something that you want to change.

4. What are you afraid of in this situation? What is the worst thing that can happen?

5. What steps are you willing to take to help change your underlying core belief?

Practices For Creation

Like the Practices for Presence, this section provides a series of practices that can be done in any order that feels right to you. Also remember that you will create your own meaning, understanding, and version of what is presented here. You may or may not connect with any particular story or example, and yet look for the messages in each section that resonate for you.

Chapter 14. Clarify and State Intention

Chapter 15. Practice Non-Attachment

Chapter 16. Be Courageous

Chapter 17. Take Wise Action

Chapter 18. Choose Love

Chapter 14.
Clarity of Intention

People of each Natural Number create their own reality by setting an intention that is likely to result in the desired outcome. It is the way that this intention setting is held that differs between Natural Numbers.

We can affect our own reality through the power of our intentionality. Getting clear on our grandest purpose and setting our intentions for our highest good allows the universe to align and create what we are here to manifest.

Our experience in the Body of 9 community is that when people get clear on their vision, and state it directly, it manifests. It is as if the universe has no choice but to assist us in manifesting our purpose. It may not always look the way it was intended, or occur in the time frame that was hoped for, but it materializes nonetheless.

Conversely, if we do not consciously create intention and make these intentions known directly and consistently to the universe, we may become an innocent bystander to other people's more conscious creations. If we abdicate our role in defining our intention, the universe does not know what to create for us. In a sense, we are ignored by the universe, and left to be bandied about by the intentions of others.

We become ruled by our belief systems and move through life competing, judging, settling, and allowing things to happen to us. In the worst-case scenario, this can result in a lifetime of victimhood and suffering. In most cases, we end up semi-content, following societal prescriptions for how we should be and what we should do.

Part of the process of growing up is to try out and embrace our role in creating the reality in which we want to live. Somewhere around the onset of puberty, many begin to have their first experiences with their spiritual nature. It might express as a sense of separation and aloneness coupled with a burgeoning awareness of one's deeper spiritual nature, or sense of oneness.

Before puberty, our parents create our reality. We live within this reality until we begin to realize we no longer need to be constrained by it. This step toward self-determination would be much easier, if we were supported in our Natural Number and encouraged to explore outside the realm of our parents' world.

Our Natural Number provides the power we need to understand that we can move toward our purpose, or our own unique path of fulfillment. Unfortunately, most children are not often encouraged to explore their spiritual nature. Instead, society intervenes, implanting the deep-seated beliefs needed in order for us to become part of the culture. The result is that we lose connection to the compass provided by our Natural Number.

Our intentions, unlike our ego-willed agendas, come from deep within. They initiate the momentum that creates our lives. Our individual intentions go toward creating the "collective intention" as well. This is what we call the Universal Field of Intention that shapes our collective reality. The Universal Field is an energy field created by our combined hopes, dreams, wishes, prayers, and intentions. Clarity of intention has large ramifications for both ourselves and for the planet, because it forms the Universal Field from which our intentions are manifested.

The manifestation process is surprisingly simple. We often think that there is some magic to manifesting our intention, or that it is only for those who have somehow "figured life out." But what if you are much more powerful than you believe? What if the process of manifestation is right at hand, built into your body?

Think about it this way: you decide you want to exercise regularly and you realize that you like to bike ride. So you set an intention to ride a bike regularly. In the simplest scenario, you buy a bike and ride it. Now you have manifested the reality you wanted to live within.

To manifest you have to take action. If you sit in your house and pine after a bike that you can't afford and decline the offer from your friend to explore new biking territory, don't expect your intention to sweep you off your feet. Taking the wise actions, described in the subsequent chapter, opens the door to all the amazing things the universe can bring to you.

This is not to say that everything intention manifests as you expected or intended. Going back to non-judgment, there is also no good or bad intention or right or wrong outcome per say. It is also true that there are many circumstances, pressures and environments in which it is not immediately possible or easy to manifest your desired intention. The point is to bring consciousness to the possibility of intention playing a role in creating your life.

We recognize that this shows up differently for each of the Natural Numbers. Manifestation and intention are skills that are understood in the context of Natural Numbers 3, 6 and 9; how do we focus, redirect, and harmonize energy flow to manifest our intention? Each of the Natural Numbers have skills and gifts that they can teach each other, to assist and guide in the conscious process of creation.

The Intention Setting Process:

1) Access yourself through your Natural Number's postural alignment. Get very clear on what you want to manifest; consider it thoroughly. Be as specific as you need to be, and as general as you want to be. Don't leave out important details, especially if they are deal breakers.

For example, once Martin and I wanted to move. We asked the universe for a rental property walking distance to school, large enough to accommodate our family, with a hot tub and a great view. We got everything we asked for, except the hot tub was rat infested and broken, and the rent was pretty high. We forgot to add affordable rent, and although we thought "working hot tub" was implicit, the universe has a sense of humor.

2) State the intention clearly and look deeper into your beliefs. People with different Natural Numbers have particular gifts that can help at different times in the transformation process.

Now is a great time to involve someone with Natural Number 3 and ask them to help clarify and articulate your intention. It is part of the Natural Number 3 superpower to help us identify and transmit our grand purpose to the Universal Field. Stating your intention clearly, out loud, lets you feel and face the hidden beliefs that might get in the way of your bigger intention. We can unwittingly create a reality that feels hard and presents challenges if we don't send clear messages to the universe.

As another example, we wanted to sell our house, pay off our debts, and find a place that could incubate Body of 9 in a healthy and supportive way. We took the required action, listed our house, and thought it would sell quickly. We had done this without a clear statement of intention. In a hot housing market, our house sat there with no one even coming to see it. We were baffled.

Then we met with our friend and coach Judy Katz. We looked at our beliefs around what we thought we deserved and our relationship with money; we found that our deeply held beliefs were unwittingly interfering with the forward progress of our larger vision. With Judy, we got clear about what was really happening and then stated our newly crafted intentions clearly. Two days later we received an offer that met all our stated intentions. It felt like a miracle; our clarity allowed the Universe to manifest what it was trying to complete.

3) Be persistent and stay with it; you don't have control. Once you have stated your intentions, "you have to keep the energy flowing". There will be actions that you have to take. In the example above, we had to release our real estate agents. They were friends, and this was hard. We held it out as the highest good for all of us. Once the energy holding the house sale from happening was addressed, it resolved quickly.

The universe seems to test our resolve. If it is a newly held intention, interesting things might start to happen that make us examine our intention. We believe this is the universe's way of asking us questions, and gauging the importance and clarity of the request.

Continuing our example, once we were in contract on selling our house we were met with a series of challenges that threatened to delay or derail the transaction. We continued to clarify our intent and dig deeper into our resistances rather than complain about how hard and unfair the process was. We found that we had to build in the capability to meet these challenges with a new response. If we retreated to our old place of victimhood, the universe would not have sufficient clarity and drive to execute the vision. Both my husband and I had to align and commit, repeatedly, then give over to the transformation process the universe was working to lay out for us. The art is to assist the process through consistent action, not to push the process artificially, and to hold out for the highest good for all involved.

Exercises for Setting Intention:

Activate yourself. Pick something that you would like to manifest; something relatively simple, but important to you. Get help from a friend—if you know someone with Natural Number 3 you can start with them.

1. Access yourself through your Natural Number's postural alignment. Get very clear on what you want to manifest, consider it thoroughly.

2. State the intention clearly out loud with your friend as witness.

3. Look deeper into your beliefs—what might stand in your way?

4. Review your intentions—did you leave something important out? Are they clear and understandable?

5. Restate any revision to your intention.

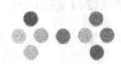

Chapter 15.

Practice Non-Attachment

Once you have set your intentions, the next step is to release attachment to how they manifest. If we are unwilling to release attachment, especially to beliefs and outcomes, we can become so focused on our own self-will that we miss the opportunities being presented by the universe. Attachment to outcome makes us prone to using the force of will that comes from our deep-seated beliefs to create the outcomes we desire. When we release outcome attachment, the universe can apply its creative paintbrush to our vision, expanding it beyond our small, ego-driven vision to include a far more beautiful and fully developed reality.

The art of setting intention to manifest your vision requires this delicate balance between being very clear on your vision and what you want to manifest, taking appropriate action without forcing or manipulating, and then allowing the universe to manifest.

Shifting your perspective to include manifesting the highest good for all in your intentions is pivotal to the creation and transformation process. It leads to an outcome that supports all of life in the process, including you. Holding out for the highest good for all also allows us to release attachment. Your next task is to trust the universe to do its work of manifestation. For those of us that like to be in control, this can be the hardest step. It is really important to understand that intention setting is not about control; it is about making a request of the universe. The rest of the job is just to notice the gifts as they fall into your lap.

If we hold tightly to one idea of what manifestation looks like, we can end up deeply disappointed with the outcome. Disappointment that results from attachment to outcome can cause us to slip into victimhood. In this place we feel powerless, sad, resigned, and all sorts of other paralyzing emotions. From this place, it can be hard to see the bigger lesson, the grander plan, or the opportunity that will present next, now that this one has not gone as expected.

When we are aware of attachments to outcome, then we can look for ways of letting them go. We notice the pain we feel, the helplessness, the anger—whatever emotion is driving us in the moment. Look a little deeper to see the disappointment, and what part of you is disappointed. Then acknowledge that you are in this place, and let it run its course for a while. Then pick yourself up, and work on changing your outlook.

• • • • • • • • •

Susan's Story: Moving On with Conscious Non-Attachment to Outcome

When we decided to move to Montana, I wanted my home to sell, so I could move as quickly as possible, before winter set in. I was excited to be free of my debts so I could begin to make the new investments to create the life I was envisioning—working full time with Martin on Body of 9.

We experienced one complication after another, which kept delaying the process. The delays that postponed the close, and were beyond my control, were the hardest for me to deal with. The complications that I could do something about had much less affect.

My attachment to the timing kept tripping me up, sending me spiraling downward into my own personal abyss. Rather than enjoy the closing and moving process, I allowed it to put me in a state of anxiety, or as my good friend Judy Katz[7] would say, it put me back in my basement room where I play the victim.

While this was going on I suffered until I was able to articulate where the pain was coming from and release it, knowing that the universe was aligning things for the highest good of all. I had to

---

[7] From Judy K. Katz, author of *Beyond Your Shadows of Doubt*.

release attachment to two particular houses that we had made offers on. I had to release the idea of buying a house and living in town. Once I released all of my attachments to how it was going to look, the universe lined it all up quite nicely. We found a property, a builder, and a temporary rental home, all in three days. We moved into our new dream house five months later.

And now that I am through to the other side, I take the learned lessons and hope to the next time I become impatient for something to happen, so that I can release my attachment to outcome and enjoy the moment to the fullest.

Exercises for Non-Attachment:

1. Think back to a time in your life when you wanted something very much. In your workbook, write down the memory of the experience: what did you want? How did you ask for it? How specific was your request? Before you found out the outcome, how did you feel? What emotions were present?

2. Did you get what you wanted?

    a. If no, once you found out that you weren't going to get what you wanted, what did you do?

    b. If yes, did it look how you expected?

3. Write down the answers to these questions:

    a. What was your emotional response?

    b. Who did you express your emotions to?

    c. What did you say to them or yourself about what this meant?

    d. What attachments did you have to this form of the outcome?

  e. How long did it take you to move on and release the attachment and disappointment?

4. Now look at what did happen. Answer these questions:

  a. What else happened as a result of not getting what you wanted?

  b. Did something else replace it?

  c. How did you feel about this alternative reality?

  d. What role did you play in creating this different outcome?

  e. How did your attachment to outcome affect your responses?

  f. What might have been different if you had released attachment to how this turned out?

5. Now, using your Observer, what do you have to say about the outcome? What did you learn? What could you do differently next time?

Chapter 16.
Be Courageous

What does Courage have to do with Presence?

In some ways courage is at the center of all change. Although courage is another word that potentially has 9 different meanings, here what we mean is using our own Natural Number specific process to move from our current state to a new, probably unknown, state of being. Courage is required for transformation. Courage is required for everything that we have been talking about in this book. The ability to witness yourself without judgment and challenge your beliefs requires the courage to view yourself with honesty and respect. Courage is the root of our self-confidence. When we bravely take the next step, despite all our stories about the possible consequences, we move, without apology, toward new possibility.

● ● ● ● ● ● ● ● ●

Susan's Practice: Leap Anyway

Each day I look at what I want to accomplish next. What is the next step in the journey I have committed to? Each day I have a choice: I can resist the growth and change awaiting me, or I can take a deep breath and leap anyway. Courage gives me the ability to leap into the unknown, to challenge all that I believe, to reset and begin anew.

Every time I stand before a person to identify their Natural Number, I have to leap. I have to show up authentically, to allow the person I am standing with to see and feel me. I have to be willing to be wrong, to make a mistake, to admit I made a mistake, and to correct the mistake if it happens. I have to be brave enough to allow someone to see me, and brave enough to see them without any judgment attached.

A few years ago, Martin and I decided to commit to Body of 9 in a new and much larger way. We realized to do so was critical to our ability to grow individually and continue to learn and develop Body of 9. This decision required us to look at everything that we were doing that stood in our way. We had to be courageous in all our choices. We chose Bozeman—our friends thought we were crazy and that we would be back after the first winter. We sold almost everything that was a part of our California life. We were creating again, almost from scratch.

I was afraid that I would lose contact with my friends, that I would be lonely in our new home, that I wouldn't be with Martin enough as we made some choices about our new life, and that I would miss my daughters. The fear had to be overcome through courage and trust in my inner wisdom.

At each step in the transition, the universe upped the ante, asking us to dig deeper and deeper into our courage. We held onto our inner wisdom, the grander vision, the deeper knowing that allowed us to decide to leap in the first place. Each time we faltered, doubted, or receded back into our fear, we took a deep breath, and connected back to each other and to the bigger vision. Courage was consistently front and center in our ability to keep leaping off the cliff.

Now we are in Bozeman, we have kept connection with our old friends, are making new friends, and are leaping off the cliff again as we step out each day, each moment, toward the bigger possibility for our purpose.

When you trust the manifestation process, magic happens. In a session with our coach we decided it was time to open a Body of 9 Center in Bozeman. Almost right away, and quite to our surprise, a location for the Body of 9 Center presented itself to us. Once we had the vision, we carefully and clearly stated our intention to make it happen, thought about what it needed to be like, and carefully established the criteria for the space and the rent.

With the onset of COVID we again had to pivot. We closed the 9 Energies Center, learned how to Identify people on-line and still provide a powerful experience. We shifted our business model and used our COVID resources to put together a team of people to help us take the next leap and create Body of 9. We again used our courage to start fresh, working toward an ever evolving vision.

● ● ● ● ● ● ● ● ●

Ashley: On Using Courage to Shift Perspective:

High school was a particularly tough time for Ashley. She often felt depressed and discouraged. For some reason, a group of kids had decided to torment and tease her. "I am a pretty regular kid. I get good grades. I play sports. I'm cute enough," she thought. "Why are they singling me out?"

Over time, the abuse took its toll and Ashley began to talk to herself in the same bullying manner. The voice in her head started to get just as mean and vile as the kids'. She became a recluse, let her friends leave her out of things, and struggled to complete her assignments, to the point where her grades started to suffer. She just wanted to stay home from school.

Her mom noticed what was happening; she always had a finger on the pulse of what was going on for her daughter. She recognized the symptoms of bullying and, sitting on Ashley's bunk bed, she settled in to talk. Ashley began by asking her mom, "What do you do when your voices tell you that you are worthless?"

"Don't believe them, and shift the thoughts," her mom replied. "Happiness is a choice; it's how you hold what happens to you. If you think the world is out to get you, and act accordingly, that is exactly what you produce for yourself. If you shift your thinking, have courage to believe in and love yourself, you can create a different reality, a more positive and loving way of being."

"Sure mom, it's that simple. You just don't understand." Ashley stalked out of the room. But something in what her mom said gave her a glimmer of hope. Perhaps she might try it.

She called her most positive friend and asked her to hang out. She decided to stop talking or trying to interact with the kids at school that weren't treating her positively. She went to talk with her teachers about her experience and her commitment to academics. She spoke positively and vulnerably, and asked them for help. As she shifted her behavior, the voices that were tearing her down quieted and she began to realize that people did like her and did want to help. Slowly and steadily, as she used her courage to create a new reality at school, her confidence grew and her depression lifted.

Exercises for Courage:

Look at the intention that you set in the prior section on Intention. Answer these questions in your workbook. Dig deep and be courageously honest with yourself:

1. Do you really want this change?

2. What stands in your way?

3. What form of courage is needed to move beyond the obstacles?

4. Where do you find this courage?

5. What help do you need to request?

Chapter 17:
Take Wise Action:

Once we make our intentions clear, taking wise action comes next. Unless I take intentional action toward my vision, nothing will change. Movement creates the dynamic needed for the transformation to manifest. There are many possible pathways available to fulfill an intention, so how do we choose?

Wise action means taking action with the most integrity, the least force, at the right time, and for the highest good of all concerned.

If we try to direct or control the outcome to our specifications, we will encounter obstacles. When we remain in integrity through the course of action and act with ease and trust, forcing nothing while still adding energy to the process, the outcomes fall into place. By choosing wise action, we can create a far better reality than that fueled solely by our ego-driven vision.

● ● ● ● ● ● ● ● ●

Susan's Story: How We got Started

In 2012, **our commitment** was born out of our first trip to Burning Man, a large festival held annually in the dessert. We were driving to the event with two Natural Number 4 friends.

The two peppered me with questions, all centered on one core question: "Why was I not willing to step out and offer what I knew and what I had learned as a gift to others? What was holding me back from living the purpose I so clearly felt in my being?" Their insistent line of questioning, and their Natural Number 4ness, took me to a new recognition of the importance of living my life from my deepest Self. They exhorted me to allow this part of me to lead.

So we arrived at Burning Man, and I was not sure where to start. What would it mean to begin? Our camp was called "Free Advice Camp, You Get What You Pay For." People with questions began stopping by when they saw our sign and wheel—you could ask the wheel a question, spin it, and it would give you an answer.

One young man was riding by on a bicycle with a cast on one leg and crutches in one hand. "That must be tough," I called out to him (Action 1). He stopped and we began a conversation about what happened. We talked for a long time.

Finally, I got up my courage and asked him if he would like to know his superpower (Action 2). I explained a bit about it, and he was excited to know.

He couldn't stand, so I worked with him sitting in a chair. The process of identifying a person's Natural Number is just a series of wise actions. I pushed gently on his shoulders to see how his body responded. I did one posture that I thought might be his. It didn't work. I noticed him closing his eyes. I invited him to bring his attention to his lower abdomen and drop inside. He went very deep, and our connection intensified. I told him what I knew about Natural Number 4, and it resonated deeply for him. Then we said goodbye. It was a rich, warm, deeply connected experience. I was on my way.

Using my courage to offer what I knew as a gift to another person opened a floodgate. He went back to his camp of skydivers and told them all about it. A group came looking for me the next day.

Then a curious person with Natural Number 2 across the way, who had been watching from the top of his RV, came over. He was blown away by what I was able to know about him. He sent his entire camp over to get identified.

I identified everyone in my camp, and they began to send their friends and people they met. This kept happening the entire week; by the end of the week, my first wise action had lead to working with fifty-six people. It was a huge leap for me. And yet that one brave action, followed by another, and another, **was the spark that** led to where we are today.

Not surprisingly, clarity of intention, courage, non-attachment—all of the Practices for Presence—were needed, and in particular, in that moment, wise action. Knowing when to act, when to wait, when to trust, and when to energize is the art of listening to yourself.

As long as I kept focused on the greatest good for all concerned, and my actions emanated from this place, the experiences of working with people moved forward smoothly and easily. Wise action stems from action in alignment with the greatest good for all. When I surrendered to my Cosmic Self, things moved forward. Whenever I asserted my needs ahead of others, things would get messy, sticky, and slow.

What are the steps, the wise actions needed to manifest any reality? Let's go back to our bicycle-riding example in the chapter on setting Intention. You want to get exercise by riding a bike. Well, first you need to own or have access to a bike. Then you need a convenient and easy place to ride the bike. If you live at the top of a steep hill, you might be less inclined to get on the bike every day because you know that at the end of the ride, you will have to climb the hill. So you need to bring in courage and either move or be ready to ride that hill.

You may not have enough money to afford a new bicycle. There are options—be open to how the bike manifests: be it trade, auction, online, or something else, investigate the options and when the universe puts the perfect bike before you, act! Don't ignore the gift just because the bike is orange and you wanted a blue one. Notice the gifts that the universe begins to place before you.

Exercises for Wise Action:

Pick an intention that you created in the section on Intentions, or a relatively simple thing that you would like to manifest. Don't start with any really tough intentions, like, "I want to lose twenty pounds," or, "I want to finish writing a book." Pick something easy and relatively achievable to start with, like returning your library books on time! You can go through this process as many times as you want.

1. Write a list of all the actions that might be needed in order to assist with manifesting the reality. Get curious: are there other ways of thinking about this intention and the way to achieve it? If you have friend with Natural Number 7, give them a call and tell them you are working on manifesting this intention. Ask them if they see any possibilities that you are missing.

2. What obstacles do you perceive are in your way? Write a list of all of the obstacles. Are there any underlying, deep-seated beliefs that you can see when you list the obstacles that will keep you from manifesting this intention?

3. If there are deep-seated beliefs in the way of manifesting this intention, circle back to the section on deep-seated beliefs to dig deeper and determine if these are beliefs that you want to change. If yes, decide how you want to address the deep-seated belief.

4. Find your courage. Take the first step. Then evaluate—how did that go? Was it easy, hard, or something in between? What obstacles showed up? Look back over our process— was your Observer active? Were you curious? Were you non-attached to how it turned out? Continue through the action steps, keeping your Observer active, and using the Practices you have learned in this book. At each step, evaluate the relative ease and the degree to which you allowed your Observer to lead your actions. How much joy did you have in the process?

5. Manifestation happens step-by-step; transformation takes a huge leap in a new direction. Sometimes the original intention was a smoke screen for what you really wanted. Is there something more here? Did things surprise you suddenly? When you take wise action and the universe does something totally unexpected, that is where the real magic lies!

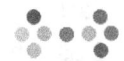

Chapter 18.

Choose Love

Love and happiness are a choice—a proactive perspective or a mantle that we can claim for ourselves.[8] While we all have emotions, and those emotional responses can exert control over our wellbeing, we also have the ability to choose a different path. Choosing love can become a habit if we practice. If our emotions are triggered by fear, for example, we can consciously choose to feel and send love toward others, thereby immediately shifting how we feel.

Each of the Natural Numbers has a different visceral experience of love. Just as the physical experience of activating a Natural Number is different for each of the nine Natural Numbers, the way that love expresses in the body is also different. Love, in fact, is the first step in feeling your Natural Number. Adjust your posture, bring attention to your movement center, activate your access to your Cosmic Self, and then consciously invite your body to send love in the direction of any thought or feeling that is disturbing you.

For example, someone with Natural Number 6 experiences their felt sense of love and wellbeing as emanating from the chest. When love is present, someone with Natural Number 4 experiences a huge sense of loving acceptance that emanates from the lower abdomen. When a person with Natural Number 5 sends love, it is accompanied by a sense of peace, clarity and ease.

---

[8] For people who suffer from mood disorders, trauma and other conditions that affect their outlook on life – we recognize that there are times when choice is not an available answer. In these cases, it is important to get the therapeutic assistance to develop new methods for coping to get to a baseline where choice begins to be available. We recognize that not everything that we are recommending in this book will work for everyone in all cases. For people, at baseline levels of healthiness combing these practices with the understanding of your Natural Number can go a long way toward understanding yourself, others and learning to create the life you want to live.

People's eyes change when they send love to others—there is a sparkle, an *aliveness*, a glimpse of the soul coming through that enables others to palpably feel love. Love calms everyone down, especially love expressed unconditionally without agenda or purpose. Express love from your body, and then **stay open to** whatever wants to happen. The more powerfully and consistently you **send** love, the more others' innate love for themselves and for you will begin to surface. When people are met with unconditional love, they are more willing to **respond with** love.

Choosing love also creates a shift in perspective that often results in a different response. The person we are interacting with finds their own higher-ground, and thus can make a more generous choice about how to be in a situation. If we choose love in all interactions, the outcomes are quite different than if we stand and hold judgment of others based on unconscious deep-seated beliefs.

As alluded to earlier, each of the Natural Numbers sends and receives love through their Activation Region. The act of sharing your wisdom and gifts is the act of sharing love. One day, in a study group, I asked everyone to actively send love to the others in the group. When I asked each person what that felt like for them, each person described the activation of their Natural Number and what it felt like to send energy from that part of their body. In that moment, it dawned on me that we use our Natural Number to express love to others.

So let's take a moment to look at how each of the Natural Numbers expresses love:

- **Natural Number 1** sends love by raising their chin and exposing the neck, thereby taking us in with their gaze and inviting us to feel the majesty of our mutual beings.

- **Natural Number 2** sends love in the form of engagement; they are always available to us for connection. Love is the sharing of connection between two bodies.

- **Natural Number 3** sends love in the form of joy from their soul, through their eyes and smile. The love they send lights up our soul, and turns on our Cosmic Self.

- **Natural Number 4** sends love by including us in their bubble, and filling that bubble with a deep sense of eternity, in which we are one, and not alone.

- **Natural Number 5** shows love in all the ways they use their empathy to ease our path through life.

- **Natural Number 6** shows love by sharing the power, aliveness, and joy of life with you, so you can know it too.

- **Natural Number 7** shows love by holding you responsible and accountable for moving toward your greatest purpose.

- **Natural Number 8** shows love in the gentleness with which they hold us, like we are a nascent shoot breaking forth through a concrete sidewalk, to be tended and cared for.

- **Natural Number 9** shows love by the way in which they hold you—all of you, no matter what part of you is showing up—and the way they catch you when you fall apart.

I suspect that the truth of this may account for a large part of the misunderstanding and disconnection we feel in the world. We do not recognize the way in which others show love to us, and we do not feel as though others receive the love we send.

Martin's Story: Commitment to Unconditional Love

I have made a personal commitment to choose unconditional love as often as I am able, in all interactions with all people. Choosing love is a moment-to-moment commitment, one that is made repeatedly with each new interaction and each new opportunity, be it within one's self, or in interaction with others.

Of course, I experience all the emotions available in our human experience. The tough ones, like anger, sadness, and frustration take me out of my strength and reduce my awareness of the current moment. I do my best to notice when I am not present in the moment. This is hard. It requires that I do everything we have talked about in this book.

The other Practices for Presence and Creation, and the other Natural Numbers, assist me with this commitment. First I bear witness to my own voice and behavior, and accept where I am. Natural Number 4 can help me feel into a place of deep self-acceptance. Learning how to generate this sense of self is a freeing feeling. Next, I get curious as to the underlying cause of my current emotions. I look at attachments, judgments, and beliefs that might be creating triggers for the emotions. Once identified, I look for a different way to respond, reset my perspective, seek the greatest good for all, and courageously take any wise action that will enable me to choose love as the energy source for interaction.

For example, recently I have changed how I handle scam calls where the person tells me that there is something wrong with my computer and I should grant them access to fix it. I used to do one of the following:

1) Hang up

2) Get mad

3) Put them on hold forever

I got a call the other day and decided to try choosing love instead. This time I began a real conversation with this person about how it felt to her to have a job where she had to lie to people all day long. I asked her how she felt. We talked about how much she needed the money. We talked about the impact on the world at large of preying on people who don't know any better. I asked her how that made her feel.

Honestly, I am not sure I had any impact on her; I probably made things harder. But in choosing to hold her with love, we at least had a real conversation about a tough subject.

● ● ● ● ● ● ● ● ●

Martin and Susan's story: Choosing Love Changed Everything

Burning Man 2012 was indeed a big year for us. The Burning Man Principles[9] presented new ways of being in community. The principles create a culture that is open, responsible, and curious.

On the final morning, a Sunday, we were invited by a camp mate to go listen to him sing in the Burning Man Choir.

Throughout the week, the message of "Choose Love" had arisen from many places. The final and most profound example came that Sunday morning, where Choose Love was the theme of the entire two-hour event. There were inspirational songs and stories that emphasized how we can interact with each other more effectively, with less stress, if we can just Choose Love in every interaction.

That night we left the event with the normal ten-hour traffic jam. Instead of feeling angered by the delay, the camaraderie of other participants, and our verbal, repeated reminder to each other to "Choose Love" made it an uplifting experience. Rather than the horrible deflating toil it could have been, we found joy in our now semi-mobile community.

No one cut in line as 30 lanes of traffic merged to one lane; people shared what they had, making coffee and handing out pancakes as we waited to begin our return to the "default world." The magic in

---

9 Burning Man co-founder Larry Harvey wrote the Ten Principles in 2001 as guidelines for the newly formed Regional Network. They were crafted as a reflection of the ethos and culture that organically developed at Burning Man. Read more here: www.burningman.org/culture/philosophical-center/10-principles/

the way we all held each other, from a place of love and non-judgment, was profound and life changing.

We have found it to be a critical ingredient in manifesting whatever we set our Cosmic Self to creating.

From then on, Choose Love has appeared in our email signatures, at the end of some of our postings, and we try to frame our lives around that simple reminder.

Choose Love is the background mantra for the Principles for Presence. Without Choosing Love, for yourself, in your relationships, and with your community, the other Principles are difficult to execute. Our Cosmic Selves are Love. We express love from our body through the region of our Natural Number. It's a choice.

Choose love.

Exercises for Choosing Love:

Until you are adept at generating and sending love through your body using your Cosmic Self, it is best to practice this with someone for whom you already feel love, and when you are not in a triggered emotional state.

> 1. **Step One:** Align your posture, activating your Natural Number if known. If not, simply find a position where you feel centered and strong. Begin to think loving thoughts toward someone; again, it is best to start with someone you actually already love.
>
> 2. **Step Two:** Find or call that person and express love to them. If in person, if it feels right, hold eye contact with them so they can see and feel the love coming from your body. If eye contact is uncomfortable for you or them, focus on the

connection from your body. Allow the interaction to become what it wants to become. Enjoy the love. Once the feeling of sending love to others is familiar in your body, you can try it in a more difficult situation.

3. **Step three:** Next time you notice yourself getting a little irritated with someone, try Step One again. For example, if the line is very long at the store and the clerk is very slow, rather than sending irritation, choose to send love—engage with the person with love. Get curious about them. Start a genuine conversation with someone in line. Use what you have learned here in the book. Be courageous and choose to send love for as long as you want. Notice the impact.

4. **Step four:** Once you have tried this a few times—including a few times where it was hard to generate the feeling of love toward someone—you will be ready when a big issue comes up with someone you love. Start with Step One, and consciously hold yourself in the place of love, no matter what the person is doing to try to trigger your emotions. Keep choosing love and sending love toward them. How is the outcome different than when you engage with them in their emotional state?

Conclusion

We believe there is an energetic source that truly supports us in achieving our defined purpose. What we wish to create gets created. We have a far greater ability to manifest from our deepest purpose than we are currently doing as human beings in the world today. Learning about our Natural Number, and developing Practices that teach us to activate our body through energetic and postural adjustments, prepares the body to learn. Adding the Practices for Presence and Creation enables us to manifest our reality in alignment with our deepest purpose, our greatest good.

When we learn to activate our Natural Number, we begin the process of witnessing, challenging, clarifying, and taking action in alignment with our deepest self. In the process, we learn how to come from unconditional love in all interactions. That decision alone will allow a paradigm shift powerful enough for us to create a new reality.

This is an iterative process that starts with the concepts presented here in this book. As you learn to activate your Natural Number, the process begins to embed itself in your body. As you learn to activate the other eight Natural Numbers in your body, your understanding of your Natural Number and the abilities associated with it become clearer. Applying courage and surrendering to the wisdom of your body creates a new clarity and understanding. Once you can actively access all nine Natural Numbers, the Observer becomes available to you as a state of being that is joyful and free of suffering.

Once awakened to our Cosmic Self, we can begin to remember how to contribute our gift and wisdom within community. We have been separated from community for so long that we have lost the ability to offer our gift to others, to listen and receive the gift of the other eight Natural Numbers. Too often, we consider our wisdom primarily in the context of our own and our immediate family's welfare, neglecting our ability to impact the larger world. And yet, this discovery about the nine Natural Numbers presents a possibility for humanity to come together in a new way. It is showing us how to build a transformative community where each of us brings forward our wisdom, receives the wisdom of the other eight, and then, in community, synthesize and create as a whole.

The task ahead isn't easy. It takes time, commitment, and repeated action to become skillful in living from your truest self for the greatest good. But what else really matters? Isn't that why we're here? So gather some friends—it is so much better to take this journey with a community—and let's get started. The world needs us, and we need us, to give our gifts. It's our time to shine.

Glossary of Terms:

Because our understanding of the Practices and Body of 9 is not devoid of beliefs, which we do our best to hold as ideas, and because language is loaded and challenging, here we define some of the terms we use in this book. Our hope and goal is to present this information as neutrally as possible so that it can be received and heard by as many people as possible.

9 Natural Numbers: Nine spiritual senses activated physically in the body.

Activation: The experience when attention is brought to one of the nine Natural Number Activation Regions through postural adjustment, attention and muscular and energetic focus, aligning and energizing the flow of the Natural Number through the body.

Body of 9, is the company founded and led by Susan and Martin Fisher whose mission is to inform, identify, and teach as many people as possible about the research and understanding presented by the Body of 9. The company is based in Bozeman, Montana. Susan and Martin operated this business under the name, *9 Energies,* from 2012 to July of 2020. The *9 Energies* organization was dissolved and Body of 9 created to take its place.

Energy Signature: Perceptible energetic feeling created when a person activates any of the nine Natural Numbers. It is perceptible to the person creating the activation and to those around who are paying attention.

Natural Number: Your principal region of the body born active and the associated way of perceiving, available to you in your body from birth that can be consciously activated by the Posture of Activation, through postural adjustment, muscular activation and intention.

Natural Number Region / Activation Region: The specific components of the skeleton, facia, and muscles that activate in a particular manner in the body for each of the Natural Numbers.

Natural Number Identification Process: A process where your body will know how to do one of nine postures, where your face will show the facial expression of activation, and where a particular energy signature will be present.

Observer: Our Observer is available when we have activated our Cosmic Self. It is a neutral place where we can observe our behavior, judgments, emotions, and belief systems without attachment, so that we can be who our being invites us to be.

Soul: Our core essence; the deepest part of ourselves that defines our greatest purpose here in this reality, and connects us back to original Source.

Transformation: The process of experimental and undirected growth, development, and learning that are orthogonal to the current direction, and not a direct extension of what is already present. Transformations are leaps in a new direction not heretofore understood.

Universal Field: An energetic field which consists of and is formed by our human experience, our collective intentions, wishes and desires, dreams, hopes, beliefs, and fears that informs the Universe—or Source of Creation—of our collective human intentions, conscious and unconscious. Body of 9 suggests that the Universal Field is what Source/the Universal energy uses to create and shape our reality and life experience.

Universe/Source: The energy or entity or source of creation that is greater than we are, provides the original energy source that powers our souls, and supports all souls in creating and having their human experience.

Universal Will: The combined intentions, hopes, dreams, and prayers of humanity that Source uses to arrange and support our collective wills here in this human manifestation on earth.

Susan's Acknowledgements

Body of 9 was birthed from a noticing about the human body and our physical experience here on earth. This connection of our physical body to our spiritual and mental nature was first explored in modern times by George Ivanovich Gurdjieff, an influential early 20th-century mystic, philosopher, spiritual teacher, and composer. There is evidence that he used scripted dances to identify people. Subsequently, the husband, and wife team Alan Sheets and Siska/Barbara Tovey, founders of New Equations, became curious about the physical aspect of the Enneagram and through their research identified the postures and facial expressions unique to each of the nine physiologically different kinds of people.

I was fortunate to be identified by New Equations as part of a leadership-training program offered by the Coaches Training Institute in 2002. This transformational experience led me to study with New Equations for the next nine years. I am forever grateful to Alan and Barbara for their support in offering the gift of community where I learned how to activate all the Natural Numbers in my body. Body of 9 could not exist without the foundation, teachings, and nurturing they provided.

I would also like to acknowledge the Coaches Training Institute. The programs offered by this wonderful organization launched my transformation from a state of confusion and despair to a state of leadership and love. Without their powerful leaders, coaches, and curriculum, I would not have become strong and prepared enough to proceed on this path. The coaches and friends who came from these programs continue to be pivotal to growing the learning expressed in this book.

Mary Reynolds Thompson, my editor, writing coach, and champion has worked with me through all the evolutions of this book. I am grateful for her tremendous writing and coaching talent, for her encouragement, and for the energy she imbues in me about the importance of the hero's journey that she and I are on together.

My children and parents need also to be acknowledged. Each has taught me so much about how to be a mother, a woman, a leader. Body of 9 and I wouldn't be what we are, but for my family.

Deep gratitude also goes to my husband and partner in all things, Martin Fisher, for his contributions to this book, and his vigilance in ensuring it passes his "Bullsh## Detector." Thank you, Martin, for your bravery and commitment, demonstrated daily in choosing to travel this path by my side. You are my magic.

About Susan Bennett Fisher

Susan, Natural Number 6, is the co-founder, with her husband, Martin Fisher, Natural Number 5, of Body of 9. She is dedicated to researching, teaching, and identifying Natural Numbers. Together they have the goal of offering this experience and understanding to as many people as possible.

Born in the United States, for the first ten years of her life Susan lived up and down the Eastern Seaboard. In 1971, her family moved to Brussels, Belgium, initiating a time of intensive travel. Susan learned French and German, and was exposed to myriad cultural perspectives and experiences that opened up her world view.

In 1982, she graduated from Brown University with a degree in Mathematical Economics and Computer Science. A member of the inaugural class of the Lauder Institute for International Business, at The Wharton School, University of Pennsylvania, Susan completed her education earning an MBA/MA in Finance and International Business. This launched a career in consulting, high-tech and finance, which brought her to Northern California in the late 1980's.

When Susan became a mother her priorities shifted. She began to question the career path she had taken. She didn't regret it exactly, but rather wondered what purpose it served in the grand scheme of life.

As Susan entered mid-life, everything, from work to family, became more of a struggle. Her priorities were shifting and exacting questions kept her up at night. She began seeking her bigger purpose—bigger than career, bigger than motherhood, bigger than simply existing. Finally, in 2002, she discovered the truth of her way of being and the source of her own inner power, and everything began to click into place.

The unusual experiences she had encountered in her youthful travels, the reason why no one in her family seemed to share her life experiences, commitments, desires, or abilities, all began to make sense. Understanding the nine Natural Numbers, Susan came home to her deepest nature.

Today, Susan is committed to researching, speaking, and learning everything about the Body of 9—how this system can help us to be happier, understand one another, work together more effectively, and know, share, and give our gifts in a way that is receivable by others. She calls it living our Cosmic Purpose, because it feels that important. And yes, that big.

For more information see the website: www.bodyof9.com

About Body of 9

Body of 9's mission is to identify as many people's Natural Number as possible and to support them to understand and apply the activation of their Natural Number.

Body of 9 is headquartered in Bozeman, Montana, run by co-founders Susan Bennett Fisher, CEO and her husband Martin R. Fisher, CTO/COO.

Body of 9 partners with Coaches and Holistic Practitioners to enhance their tools and offerings. Imagine what it would be like to have an almost automatic ability to quickly build lasting relationship – or that you could ensure your process will give clients effective and long-lasting results. The Body of 9 system helps you bypass the layers of nurture, going straight to the nature of your client so that you can coach with laser precision and ease in a way that your client feels seen and heard.

Susan and Martin are available to travel to conferences, festivals, and other large gatherings, speaking about and offering the Body of 9 identification experience.

If you would like to bring Body of 9 to your community, contact us at info@bodyof9.com or via phone at (406) 577-6553.

For more information see the website: bodyof9.com

www.ingramcontent.com/pod-product-compliance
Lightning Source LLC
LaVergne TN
LVHW051524070426
835507LV00023B/3290